The
Gingerbread Lady

A New Play

by Neil Simon

A SAMUEL FRENCH ACTING EDITION

SAMUEL
FRENCH

FOUNDED 1830

New York Hollywood London Toronto

SAMUELFRENCH.COM

ISBN   978-0-573-60935-0   Printed   in   U.S.A.   #478

MUSIC USE NOTE

Licensees are solely responsible for obtaining formal written permission from copyright owners to use copyrighted music in the performance of this play and are strongly cautioned to do so. If no such permission is obtained by the licensee, then the licensee must use only original music that the licensee owns and controls. Licensees are solely responsible and liable for all music clearances and shall indemnify the copyright owners of the play and their licensing agent, Samuel French, Inc., against any costs, expenses, losses and liabilities arising from the use of music by licensees.

IMPORTANT BILLING AND CREDIT REQUIREMENTS

All producers of *THE GINGERBREAD LADY must* give credit to the Author of the Play in all programs distributed in connection with performances of the Play, and in all instances in which the title of the Play appears for the purposes of advertising, publicizing or otherwise exploiting the Play and/or a production. The name of the Author *must* appear on a separate line on which no other name appears, immediately following the title and *must* appear in size of type not less than fifty percent of the size of the title type.

THE GINGERBREAD LADY was first presented, December 13, 1970, at the Plymouth Theatre, New York City, by Saint-Subber. It was under the direction of Robert Moore. The following were the members of the original cast:

CAST OF CHARACTERS

(In Order of Appearance)

JIMMY PERRY .... *Michael Lombard*

MANUEL .... *Alex Colon*

TOBY LANDAU .... *Betsy von Furstenberg*

EVY MEARA .... *Maureen Stapleton*

POLLY MEARA .... *Ayn Ruymen*

LOU TANNER .... *Charles Siebert*

ACT ONE

A Brownstone Apartment in the West Seventies

Mid-November—Late Afternoon

ACT TWO

Three Weeks Later—About 9:00 P.M.

ACT THREE

The Following Morning

The Gingerbread Lady

ACT ONE

SCENE: *The third floor apartment in a brownstone in the West Eighties. It consists of a living room, a bedroom and, to L., a kitchen. The rooms are fairly large with high ceilings and what were once very nice wood panelings but now painted over. In the mid-thirties and forties this was a great place to live. The furniture is very good and probably very attractive, but one could hardly tell anymore. It has fallen into disrepair. There is a small, battered piano against the wall which is filled with photographs, all of a theatrical nature. A stack of mail is on table.*

AT RISE: *A man's sheepskin coat is draped over a chair. From the kitchen we hear the faucet running and a MAN humming. He comes out with a vase of freshly filled flowers. JAMES PERRY is in his early forties, portly and probably homosexual. Probably but not obviously. He wears slacks with a dark-blue turtleneck sweater. He first crosses to window, peers out and down, looking for the arrival of someone, then turns back in and looks for a place to put vase. He tries the piano, changes his mind, then settles on the coffee table. It doesn't please him much.*

JIMMY. I hate it. (*The DOORBELL rings. Looks at his watch nervously. Crosses to door and asks without opening:*) Who is it?
VOICE. Groceries.

(JIMMY *opens door and glares at the* DELIVERY BOY,

5

Spanish and about twenty, with two large grocery bags in his arms.)

JIMMY. Where were you? I thought you went out of business. . . . Put them in the kitchen, please.

BOY. (*At doorway.*) Mrs. Meara live here?

JIMMY. Yes, Mrs. Meara lives here. Would you please put them in the kitchen.

BOY. (*Not moving.*) Is fourteen dollars twenny-eight cents.

JIMMY. Fine. Terrific. That's a charge. Just put them in the kitchen. (*Starts to walk away, but notices that the* BOY *is not moving.*)

BOY. Mr. D'Allessandro say to me I mus' have fourteen dollars and twenny-eight cents.

JIMMY. No, you don't understand. Mrs. Meara has a charge account. *Charge—account!* Do you know what that is?

BOY. (*Nods.*) Tha's a charge account.

JIMMY. That's right. It's an account and you charge it. I don't live here. I'm a friend of Mrs. Meara. You charge it to her account.

BOY. Mr. D'Allessandro say to me eef they say to you, eet's a charge account, you say to them eet's fourteen dollars and twenny-eight cents.

JIMMY. Do you want me to get on the phone and call Mr. D'Allessandro? . . . What's the number?

BOY. The number? The telephone number? Ees seven six six something, I don't know, I never call them. . . . Eef you speak to Mr. D'Allessandro he's gonna say to you eet's fourteen dollars and twenny-eight cents.

JIMMY. (*Irritated.*) I don't have to call Food Fair, you know. They have canned goods in Bohacks, too.

BOY. Bohacks is nice. My cousin works for Bohacks. They all the same, you know.

JIMMY. (*Glares at* BOY.) . . . I don't have fourteen dollars and twenty-eight cents. I have no money on me.

BOY. Oh, well, tha's okay. I'm sorry. (*Turns.*)

JIMMY. Where are you going?

BOY. Back to Mr. D'Allessandro.

JIMMY. Wait a minute. I'll look. (*Takes out his wallet from back pocket. The* BOY *smiles at him.* JIMMY *turns his back so the* BOY *can't see into his wallet. Takes out one bill.*) I have ten dollars.

BOY. (*Shrugs.*) . . . I leave you one package.

JIMMY. (*Glares more angrily.*) Wait here. (*Starts for his sheepskin coat, notices that the* BOY *has edged inside a step or two.*) That's far enough.

BOY. Wha's a matter, meester, you afraid I come inside, I rob you house? I don' rob no houses.

JIMMY. I don't care what you do, just wait there.

BOY. I got a good job, I don' have to rob houses.

JIMMY. (*Half to himself as he goes through his pockets.*) Yeah, in the daytime. (*Takes passbook out of pocket and some loose dollar bills. Holds book in one hand and counts money as he crosses back.*) How much was that again?

BOY. Same thing, fourteen dollars twenny-eight cents. (BOY *puts the bags down.* JIMMY *takes out four singles, hands them to* BOY, *but in the process he drops the passbook on table. The* BOY *picks it up, looks at it.*) Oh, I use to have thees. Unemployment book. You unemployed, meester?

JIMMY. (*Grabs it back.*) None of your damned business. Who asked you? You've got your fourteen dollars, you can leave now.

BOY. (*Holds out hand.*) And twenny-eight cents.

JIMMY. (*Reaches into his pocket and takes out change. Hands it to* BOY, *one coin at a time.*) Ten . . . fifteen, twenty-five, twenty-six, twenty-seven, twenty-eight cents. (BOY *looks at it, nods his head in agreement.*) . . . That's all. There's no tip. I don't live here. I don't tip where I don't live.

BOY. I don' wan' no tip. You ain't even got a job, I don' need your tips.

JIMMY. And I don't need your Goddamned sympathy. You're very fresh for a delivery boy.

BOY. Wha's a matter, you don' like Spanish people?

JIMMY. Who the hell said anything about Spanish people? *You're* the only one I don't like. Will you please leave now.

BOY. (*At the door.*) I know the kind of people *you* like, meester. (*Makes two kissing sounds with his pursed lips.*)

JIMMY. *Get out of here!!* (*The* BOY *smiles and rushes out, the door closing behind him. . . .* JIMMY *bolts door, then crosses to the grocery bags, still fuming.*) . . . I wouldn't live in this neighborhood if you paid me. . . . (*Picks up the bags and starts for the kitchen.*) Can't say a thing anymore, everyone is so Goddamned race conscious. . . . Lousy spic! (*Goes into the kitchen. We hear the rustle of the paper bags as the PHONE RINGS.* JIMMY *comes out with a can of coffee in his hand and crosses to the phone.*) Hello? . . . No, she's not, I'm expecting her home any minute. Who's calling, please? . . . Well, in regards to what? . . . Oh! Well, I'm sure Mrs. Meara hasn't not paid her phone bill intentionally, she's been away sick for the past ten weeks. . . . But you're not going to cut it off, are you? She'll pay it as soon as she gets home. . . . Fourth notice already, my goodness. . . . But you must realize she's good for it, I mean this is Evelyn Meara, the singer. . . . It must be in by Tuesday, yes, I'll tell her that. Thank you very much, I appreciate that. (*Hangs up. To the phone:*) Wait three years to get one but you rip 'em out fast enough, don't you? (*Continues opening the can. The FRONT DOOR-BELL RINGS.* JIMMY *turns and looks at the door. He is extremely anxious. Puts the can of coffee down on chair, wipes his hands on his pants and crosses to door. Calls out without opening.*) Who is it?

WOMAN'S VOICE. It's us. We're home.

(JIMMY *tries to open door but it doesn't work since he's*

forgotten that he bolted it. Tries to unbolt it but has a little difficulty at first.)

JIMMY. (*Calls out.*) Wait a second, I'm so damned nervous. (*Finally opens it and* TOBY LANDAU *enters, a very pretty woman in her early forties, but you'd never believe it. That's because she spends most of her waking hours trying to achieve that effect. She is well dressed in a smartly tailored suit. She carries a large, heavy, but not very elegant suitcase.*) Look at me, I'm shaking.

TOBY. (*Entering.*) Don't complain to me. I just spent four hours in a taxi on the Long Island Expressway. Look out the window, you'll see a very rich cab driver. (*Looks around the apartment.*)

JIMMY. Where is she? (*Looks out door.*) Evy? Where's Evy?

TOBY. She's saying hello to a neighbor. . . . I thought you were going to clean the apartment. Didn't you say you would clean the apartment for Evy?

JIMMY. I tried rearranging the furniture, but it always came out like a bus terminal in Passaic. Where is she? Is she alright?

TOBY. Yes, but you're going to be shocked when you see her. She lost 42 pounds.

JIMMY. Oh, my God.

TOBY. I will tell you right here and now that a rest home for drunks is the most depressing place in the world.

JIMMY. I never thought she'd last it out. I'm so nervous. What do I say to her? How do I act in front of her?

TOBY. You hug her and love her and, above all, you must trust her.

JIMMY. I'll kill her if she ever takes another drink. . . . Where the hell is she?

(*We hear* EVY'S *voice just outside the door.*)

EVY. (*Offstage.*) I'm out in the hall. Are you ready?
JIMMY. Ready.

(Evy *enters, in mink coat and carrying books.*)

Evy. Alright, say it, I'm gorgeous, right?

Jimmy. Oh, my God, I don't believe it. Who is she? Who is this beautiful woman?

Evy. It better be me or I'm out twenty-seven hundred bucks.

Jimmy. Am I allowed to hug you?

Evy. You're allowed.

Jimmy. (*Rushes into her arms and hugs her. He feels her.*) It's true. It's gone. Forty-two pounds are gone. Where did it go to?

Evy. You want it? It's in the suitcase.

Jimmy. I can't get over it. It's like talking to a stranger. Somebody introduce me.

Toby. Jimmy, this is Evelyn Meara. Remember? She used to sing in clubs?

Jimmy. That fat lady? Who used to drink a lot? Use foul language? No. This is a nice, skinny woman. You put a dress on her, you can take her anywhere.

Evy. I don't want to go anywhere. I want to be right here in my own apartment. . . . Oh, it's so good to be home. (*Looks around.*) Jesus, it looks different when you're sober. I thought I had twice as much furniture.

Toby. Will you sit down? She won't sit down. She stood all the way in the taxi coming home.

Jimmy. You must be starved. When did you eat last?

Evy. I had chicken salad in July. I'm not hungry.

Toby. The doctors told me she worked harder than any patient there. Even the nurses were so proud of her.

Evy. It's the truth. I was the best drunk on my floor. . . . (*Looking at sectional.*) Christ, now it's coming back to me. I threw the other half of this out the window.

Jimmy. I want to make you something. Let me make you a tongue and Swiss on toast and a pot of coffee. Sit down. I'll be five minutes.

Evy. I thought my mother lived in Ohio. Leave me alone. I tortured myself to lose 42 pounds.

TOBY. Jimmy, stop it, you'll get Evy nervous.

JIMMY. I'm worried about her. If someone doesn't make it for her she doesn't eat.

EVY. There's plenty of time to eat next year. I'm alright. I'm home. Let me enjoy myself.

JIMMY. Who's stopping you? (*To* TOBY . . . *softly:*) She look alright to you? (TOBY *nods*.) Is there anything she has to take? Pills or anything?

TOBY. Just some tranquilizers. She has them in her bag.

JIMMY. But nothing heavy? No serious stuff?

TOBY. Just a mild sedative to help her sleep.

EVY. (*At kitchen door.*) If you doctors want to be alone, I can go back to Happy Valley. . . . What are you whispering about?

JIMMY. We're not whispering. We're talking softly.

EVY. You were whispering.

JIMMY. We were not whispering. We were talking softly.

EVY. Why were you talking softly?

JIMMY. Because we don't want you to hear what we're saying. . . .

TOBY. Jimmy's worried about you, that's all.

EVY. If he's worried, let him worry a little louder. I can't stand whispering. Every time a doctor whispers in the hospital, the next day there's a funeral.

JIMMY. I'm sorry. I'm sorry.

EVY. It took ten weeks to cure me and five minutes for you to drive me crazy.

TOBY. Jimmy didn't mean it, darling.

EVY. What are you blaming him? You were whispering too.

TOBY. I had to. He whispered a question to me.

JIMMY. Alright, can we drop it?

TOBY. I didn't even bring it up.

EVY. Jesus, I got along better with the nuts on Long Island.

JIMMY. I'm sorry, Evy. Alright? I'm nervous I'm gonna

say the wrong thing. I don't know how to act in front of somebody who just got home from the cure five minutes ago.

Evy. You act natural. The way you always acted with me.

Jimmy. This is the way I always acted with you.

Evy. Yeah? Well, maybe that's why I started to drink.

Toby. My God, what a homecoming!

Evy. (*Wilts a little.*) Hey, listen, I'm sorry. Maybe I am nervous. . . . Don't pay attention to me. Jimmy, you know what I'd love more than anything else in the world? A tongue and Swiss on toast and a pot of coffee.

Jimmy. Do you mean it?

Evy. I dreamt of it every night. First I dreamt of **sex**, then a tongue and Swiss on toast.

Jimmy. I'll bring you the sandwich. The rest I can't help you with. (*Exits into kitchen.*)

Toby. (*Looking at herself in mirror.*) And what can I do, Evy?

Evy. You can stop looking at yourself and give me a cigarette.

Toby. You *are* nervous, aren't you?

Evy. I hated that place so much I used to save up matches planning to burn it down. It was a Goddamn prison. And then when it came time to leave I was afraid to go. . . . I suddenly felt comfortable there. . . . Can I have my cigarette, please?

Toby. That's almost a whole pack since we left the hospital. Are you sure they said it's alright to smoke?

Evy. Once you pay your bill and check out, they don't care if you get knocked up by a dwarf. (*Takes cigarette and smokes.*) I thought I'd have a million things to do once I got home. I'm here six minutes, I'm bored to death.

Toby. You've got to give yourself time, Evy. And then you're going to start your life all over again and you're going to grow up to be a beautiful wonderful person like me.

Evy. What's that? What's that crap you're putting on your face?

Toby. It's a special crap that protects the skin. Have you noticed you've never seen pores on me. As long as you've known me, have you ever seen a single pore on my face?

Evy. I've never even seen your face. . . . Who are you anyway?

Toby. A woman can never be too pretty. It's her feminine obligation. I love my looks, don't you?

Evy. You're gorgeous. If you went bald and lost your teeth, you'd still be cute looking. Leave yourself alone.

Toby. I can't. Isn't it terrible? I'm obsessed.

Evy. You remind me of the psycho in the room next to me. She used to shampoo her eyelashes every night. Thought all the doctors were in love with her. An eighty-seven-year-old virgin screwball.

Toby. What a sweet story. You just going to sit there forever? Aren't you going to unpack or something?

Evy. Unpack what? A pair of pajamas and a bottle of mineral oil? Besides, I'm never going in that bedroom again. I ruined half my life in there, the next half I'm playing it safe.

Toby. I understand perfectly. But how will you get to the bathroom?

Evy. Over the roof and down the pipes. Just worry about your face, alright?

Toby. I can worry about both. I wish I could stay with you tonight.

Evy. Then why don't you stay with me tonight?

Toby. I have to meet Martin at Pavilon for dinner. It's business, I distract the client.

Evy. Some friend you are.

Toby. Don't say it like that. I'm a wonderful friend. I'm sensitive. You want me to be hurt?

Evy. Don't pout. You'll crack your makeup and start an avalanche on your face.

Toby. Anyway Jimmy can stay with you tonight.

JIMMY. (*Sticks head through kitchen window.*) Jimmy
has an audition at five forty-five.

TOBY. You said you'd be free tonight.

JIMMY. I was until the audition came up. I have to eat,
you know.

TOBY. Can't you cancel it? For Evy?

JIMMY. I wouldn't cancel it for Paul Newman.

TOBY. Oh, God, Evy, I'm sorry. What will you do tonight?

EVY. I'll turn on television and stand stark naked in
front of Merv Griffin. What the hell do you think I'm
going to do all alone?

TOBY. You could call Polly. She's probably home from
school by now.

EVY. I'm not ready to see my daughter yet, thank you.
What I'd really like to do is move the hell out of this
dump.

TOBY. Then why don't you move?

EVY. Because, dumb dumb, I still pay a hundred and
twenty dollars for three and a half rooms. It's on a sublet
from Mary Todd Lincoln.

TOBY. You can borrow from Marty and me until you
go back to work again.

EVY. Work? Singing in clubs? The last job I had was
two years ago in Pittsburgh. I broke the house record.
Fell off the stool seventeen times in one show.

TOBY. That's old news, I don't want to hear about it.

EVY. I shared a dressing room with a female imper-
sonator who had the hots for me. I think we made it but
I forget which way.

TOBY. You don't have to sing in clubs. There's television, Martin knows people in advertising. You can be a
cat in a tuna fish commercial, you'll make a fortune. . . .
I've got to go.

EVY. So soon?

TOBY. I'm afraid so. Marty's waiting.

EVY. Just gonna dump me here like a basket case, heh?
I thought you were going to stay and grow old with me.

TOBY. Don't be silly. I'm never growing old. . . . I won't go if you're really desperate.

EVY. When have you known me when I wasn't desperate?

TOBY. Never. If you need me I'll be at Martin's office and then at Pavilon. Can I send you anything?

EVY. How about the headwaiter?

TOBY. Armand? He doesn't go for women.

JIMMY. (*Entering with tray of coffee.*) Send him anyway, we'll find something for him to do.

TOBY. Evy, this may be one of the happier days of my life.

EVY. Toby, if you didn't come pick me up today . . .

TOBY. I told you. I'm always way the hell out on Long Island early Thursday mornings. Tell me once more how pretty I am.

EVY. Helen of Troy couldn't carry your compact.

TOBY. I believe you, Evelyn. I really do. I'll call you from the restaurant. (*Crosses to door, stops.*) Evy . . . say it just once more.

EVY. Say what?

TOBY. What you promised me in the taxi.

EVY. . . . I will be a good girl. Forever and ever.

TOBY. Oh, Christ, I'm going to cry; there goes my makeup. (*Exits quickly and* EVY *turns to* JIMMY.)

JIMMY. You skinny bastard, I'm so proud of you.

EVY. Is that why you didn't visit me once in ten weeks?

JIMMY. I can't go to hospitals, you know that. I pass out in hospitals. If I ever get hit by a car I tell them, "Take me to a drug store, never a hospital."

EVY. It wasn't a hospital. It's a sanitarium for drunks.

JIMMY. They had white shoes and cotton balls, that's enough for me. (*Hands her coffee cup.*) Didn't I call you almost every day? Didn't I send you popular novels?

EVY. Queen Alexandra and her hemophiliac son? Couldn't you send me a sex manual, for crise sakes.

JIMMY. I'm sorry I was nice to you. Next time I'll just send you a get sober telegram.

Evy. How much do I owe you for the groceries?

Jimmy. We got 'em free. I had an affair with the delivery boy.

Evy. Next time *I'll* answer the door. Give me the bill.

Jimmy. Don't be ridiculous. Where would I get money?

Evy. You were just in a show.

Jimmy. That was in October and we ran two nights and were closed by the police. Please don't ask me what I had to do naked with six people on the stage.

Evy. Was it something sexual?

Jimmy. I couldn't tell, I had my eyes closed. . . . That is the Goddamned last time I will ever take my clothes off in public. Not only have I not worked since then, I can't even get a lousy date anymore. You know what I did to keep alive? God is my judge, I worked in Bonwit's selling snakeskin toilet-seat covers, on my mother's life.

Evy. (*At window, looking out.*) I don't see any men on the streets. Little boys, fags, hippies, but no men.

Jimmy. What kills me is that I'm so good. I'm such a good actor I can't stand it. But I'm too late. Show business is over this year. There will be no more entertainment in the world after June. Maybe you'll see a person whistling or humming on the street, but that's all. I was born too talented and too late. What are you doing at the window? Who are you looking for?

Evy. Nothing.

Jimmy. You look tired. Why don't you lie down for a while?

Evy. I don't want to lie down.

Jimmy. You've got to lie down sometime.

Evy. That's an old wives' tale. I've known people to stand for years at a time. . . .

Jimmy. (*Lost in his own problems.*) I won't get this job tonight. They'll turn me down. I'm auditioning for some nineteen-year-old putz producer who has seventy-five thousand dollars and a drama degree from Oklahoma A & M. . . . First time he walked into the theatre he fell off the stage, broke two ribs . . . some chance an intelli-

gent actor has today. . . . Oh God, I want to be a star
so bad. Not a little star. I want to be a big star with three
agents and two lawyers and a business manager and a
press agent and then I'd fire all of them and get new ones
because I'm such a big star. And I'd make everyone pay
for the twenty-two years I poured into this business. I
wouldn't do benefits, I wouldn't give money to charity.
I would become one of the great shitheels of all time.
Isn't that a wonderful dream, Evy?

Evy. (*Looks around.*) She didn't leave any cigarettes.
Stupid dumb broad.

Jimmy. (*Takes crumpled pack out of shirt pocket.*)
Here. Take whatever I have. My money, my blood, whatever you want, only calm down because I don't trust you
when you get nervous.

Evy. I just made up my mind, I don't like you. (*Takes
one of the cigarettes.*)

Jimmy. You never liked me. For fifteen years it's been
a one-sided friendship. I'm the one who always worries
about you, picks you up off the floor, puts you to bed,
feeds you . . . and for what? Christmas you gave me the
one lousy album you made in 1933. . . . Well, I'm
through. I can't take it anymore. You're skinny and sober,
take care of yourself now.

Evy. How'd you like a big wet kiss on the mouth?

Jimmy. How'd you like a tongue and Swiss on toast?
Sit down, it's ready. (*Starts for kitchen.*)

Evy. (*Yells.*) Jimmy, will you stay here and talk to
me!

Jimmy. (*Stops.*) What do you want to talk about?

Evy. Anything, dammit, pick a subject.

Jimmy. Why don't you ask me, Evy? Why don't you
get it over with and *ask me?* . . . No, I have not seen
him or spoken to him, alright?

Evy. (*Pause . . . nods.*) Alright.

Jimmy. I'm lying. I saw him at the bar in Downey's
last week. I don't think he's doing well because he had
one beer and ate all the pretzels in the dish. . . .

EVY. Was he alone?

JIMMY. Yes. I know because when he left I watched him through the window, hoping he'd get hit by the Eighth Avenue bus. . . . What else do you want to know?

EVY. Nothing. I was curious, not interested.

JIMMY. Oh, really? Is that why you keep staring out the window? Is that why you won't go into the bedroom? What are you afraid of, you'll see his lousy ghost sitting on the john doing the *Times* crossword puzzle? . . . Go on. Go in the bedroom and get it over with, for crise sakes. (EVY *looks at him, then crosses into bedroom. It is quiet a moment. Then we hear* EVY *from bedroom.*)

EVY. How'd you get the Bloody Mary stains off the wallpaper?

JIMMY. I hung your bathrobe over them.

EVY. You know what I'll do? I'll repaint the room white. The whole bedroom white, top to bottom. Walls, floors, bedspreads, shoes, stockings, everything white. And I'm going to forget everything that ever happened in there and I'm going to become one happy, TV-watching, Protestant square-assed lady, how about that?

JIMMY. Nixon'll be thrilled.

(*The DOORBELL RINGS.* EVY *looks startled.*)

EVY. Are you expecting anyone?

JIMMY. I don't even live here. Should I answer it? They're just going to ring again. (*IT RINGS AGAIN.*) See!

(EVY *nods. He opens door. It's the* SPANISH DELIVERY BOY *with one package in arms.*)

BOY. I forget the soda. Six cans Coca-Cola, six cans Canada Dry Ginger Ale. Two dollars, forty cents.

JIMMY. I paid you before, didn't I? (*Tries to grab package.*)

BOY. You paid me for las' time, you din't pay me for this time. Two dollars and forty cents, please.

JIMMY. (*Angry.*) Did you tell D'Allessandro that Mrs. Meara is going to take her business somewhere else?

BOY. He don' care. He say "Take the Coca-Cola somewhere else."

EVY. (*Steps forward.*) What's wrong?

JIMMY. There's nothing wrong. (*To* BOY.) Wait out there, I'll get your money. (*Takes bag, crosses into kitchen.*)

BOY. I don' wanna come in your house.

EVY. (*Steps out into* C. *of room so that she is in view of the* BOY *for the first time.*) Jimmy, don't leave him out in the hall like that. (*To* BOY.) That's alright, you can come in.

BOY. (*Looks at her and smiles back.*) Oh. Okay. (*Steps in.*)

EVY. (*Smiles at* BOY.) I'm Mrs. Meara.

BOY. Oh, yes? Hello, Mrs. Meara, nice to meet you. (*Nods his head a few times, looks her up and down.*) I brought you six cans Coca-Cola, six cans Canada Dry Ginger Ale. Okay?

EVY. I don't see why not. That's a charge. And put fifty cents on for yourself.

BOY. Oh, thank you very much.

EVY. You're welcome.

BOY. But I need two dollars, forty cents. Mr. D'Allessandro say to me—

EVY. I know what Mr. D'Allessandro said to you. It's alright. You tell him Mrs. Meara is home and will take care of everything by check again. Will you do that?

BOY. Yes. I'm going to tell him that. But he's going to tell me not to tell him that.

EVY. What's your name?

BOY. Mr. D'Allessandro.

EVY. No, *your* name.

BOY. *My* name? You want to know *my* name? Manuel.

EVY. Manuel?

BOY. (*Nods.*) Manuel. Yes, that's my name. Manuel. Eet's Spanish.

(JIMMY *comes out of kitchen.*)

EVY. I haven't seen you before, Manuel. What happened to the other boy?

BOY. Pablo? Pablo got married and is now work in a better job. Bloomingdale's.

EVY. Really? He seemed so young.

BOY. They don' care how old you are in Bloomingdale's.

EVY. I mean to get married.

BOY. Oh. Pablo is twenny years old, same as me.

EVY. You're twenty?

(JIMMY *has been watching this with consternation.*)

BOY. Tha's me, twenny.

EVY. Well, let's hope that you get married and find a better job too, Manuel.

BOY. Eet's okay eef I find a better job but I don' wanna get married. I'm okay now, you know what I mean?

EVY. (*Smiles.*) You mean you have lots of girl friends, is that it?

BOY. Sure. Why not?

EVY. Well, you tell Mr. D'Allessandro I will send him his check the first thing every month. Will you do that?

BOY. The first thing every month. Tha's what I'm gonna tell him.

EVY. And put fifty cents on for yourself. I don't have any change just now.

BOY. Tha's awright. . . . I come again—you take care of me another time—you know what I mean? (*Has a slight implication in his meaning that does not go unnoticed by* EVY *or* JIMMY.) Goo'bye, Mrs. Meara. (*To* JIMMY.) Okay, meester, it's okay now, we're good friends again, alright? (*Winks at* JIMMY *and exits, closing the door behind him.*)

JIMMY. (*Yells.*) Jesus Christ! Why didn't you invite him in to listen to your Xavier Cugat records. Are you crazy?

EVY. Oh, come on, he's a delivery boy.

JIMMY. I saw the look he gave you and I know what he wants to deliver.

EVY. I'm not in *that* kind of trouble yet. . . . Maybe in a few weeks, but not yet.

JIMMY. I can't trust you. I can't trust you alone for ten minutes.

EVY. I can be trusted for ten minutes.

JIMMY. I know you, Evy. I wouldn't leave you with the Pope during Holy Week. . . . Haven't you had enough trouble this year?

EVY. I've had enough for the rest of my life. For Christ's sake, I'm not going to shack up with a delivery boy. I don't even have a quarter to give him a tip.

JIMMY. You'll charge it like everything else.

EVY. Oh, God, Jimmy, I really love you. You don't know how good it is to have somebody worried about you.

JIMMY. Well, I hate it. I have enough trouble worrying about me. I'm forty years old and I can't get a job with or without clothes anymore. If you want to carry on with Pancho Gonzales, that's up to you.

EVY. (*Puts arms around* JIMMY.) . . . Of all the stinking people in this world, you sure ain't one of them.

JIMMY. Well, I'm glad you finally realize all the others are stinking.

EVY. Why don't you marry me?

JIMMY. Because you're a drunken nymphomaniac and I'm a homosexual. We'd have trouble getting our kids into a good school.

EVY. Give me a kiss. (*He kisses her lightly.*) Come on. Give me a real kiss. Who the hell's gonna know? (*He kisses her with feeling.*)

JIMMY. God will punish us for the terrible thing we're doing.

EVY. Don't get depressed, but you get me very excited.

JIMMY. I don't have to stay and listen to this kind of talk (*Breaks away from her.*) I've got to go. If you promise to behave yourself, I may be nice to you when I'm a star.

EVY. We could live together in Canada. They don't do sex in Canada.

JIMMY. (*Putting on his bag.*) Stop it, Evy, you're confusing my hormones. I'm late.

EVY. Jimmy!

JIMMY. (*Stops.*) What?

EVY. Nothing. I just love you and want to thank you for being here today.

JIMMY. Don't thank me, just pray for me. Pray that I get this show because I think it's the last one in the world.

EVY. Will you call me the minute you hear anything?

JIMMY. It's off-Broadway, there are no phones. (*On his way out.*) I bought you that Stouffers macaroni that you love. And some Sara Lee cheesecake. And I made you enough coffee until February. . . . Will you remember to drink it?

EVY. Drinking is one thing I remember.

JIMMY. And get some sleep.

EVY. I promise.

JIMMY. And if Jose Ferrer shows his face again, don't open the door. The only groceries he's bringing next time are his own. (*Exits, closing the door behind him. Evy turns and looks at the empty apartment with full realization that she is alone, alone for the first time again in months. She picks up her suitcase and literally throws it into the bedroom.*)

EVY. Alright, don't panic, we'll take it one night at a time. (*Looks around, puffs up pillows on sofa, then sits on the sofa.*) . . . And that's it for the week! (*Crosses to piano, plays a few notes of "Close to You," then sings the first line.*) . . . Thank you, thank you. . . . For my next number, Ed Sullivan and I will make it right here on this stage. . . . (*Sighs heavily. She is fighting to keep from losing control of herself. Looks at the phone, crosses to it quickly, sits and dials. . . . Into phone:*) Hello? . . . Is Miss Meara there? . . . No, not *Mrs.* Meara, *Miss!* . . . Oh? How long ago? . . . Well, when she gets in, would you please tell her— (*Suddenly a key opens the lock and the front door opens.* POLLY MEARA *stands there with one large heavy suitcase.* POLLY *is 17, pretty, with long straight hair and no pretensions. She wears blue jeans, a sweater and a jacket. There is a long and emotional pause as the two stare at each other across the room. Then* EVY *speaks into the phone.*) Never mind, I just heard from her. (*Hangs up and stares at* POLLY.)

POLLY. I don't want to get your hopes up, but I have reason to believe I'm your daughter!

EVY. No, you're not. *My* daughter would have called first. . . . (*No longer able to contain herself.*) You rotten kid, you want to give me a heart attack? (*They rush to each other, arms around each other in a huge, warm embrace.* EVY *squeezes her tightly.*) Oh, God, Polly, Polly . . .

POLLY. I was hoping I'd get here before you. But I was late getting out of school. Of all damn days . . . (*They break the embrace.* EVY *wipes her eyes.*)

EVY. Okay, I'm crying. You satisfied? You just destroyed a helpless old woman. . . . Well, why the hell aren't you crying?

POLLY. I'm too happy. I can't believe it. My God, look at you.

EVY. What do you think?

POLLY. You're gorgeous. Skinniest mother I ever had. I can wear your clothes now.

EVY. What size dress do you wear?

POLLY. Five.

EVY. Tough, kid, I wear a four. (*Wipes teary eyes again.*) Damn, I knew this would happen. You weren't supposed to know I was home. I needed three days before I could face you.

POLLY. I called the hospital this morning. You didn't think I could wait, did you?

EVY. Neither could I. Oh, God, give me another hug, I can't stand it. (*They embrace.*) Alright, if we're going to get physical, let's close the door. There's enough talk about me in this building. (*Closes the door.* POLLY *crosses and gets the suitcase out of the doorway.*)

POLLY. I'll get that. (*Picks it up.*)

EVY. Have you had dinner yet?

POLLY. I haven't even had lunch. I was too nervous.

EVY. I just loaded up for the winter. We'll have a food festival. Come on, take your coat off, let me look at you. Hey, what'd you do with your hair?

POLLY. Nothing.

EVY. I know. It's been three months, when you gonna do something?

POLLY. Don't bug me about the way I look. I'm not that secure yet. (*Picks up suitcase, heads for bedroom.*)

EVY. I should have your problems. Where you going with that?

POLLY. In the bedroom.

EVY. What is it?

POLLY. (*Looks at it.*) Looks like a suitcase.

EVY. Thanks, I was wondering. What's in the suitcase?

POLLY. (*Shrugs.*) Dresses, shoes, books, things like that.

EVY. Why do you have things like that in your suitcase?

POLLY. Well, otherwise they fall on the floor.

EVY. Alright, no one likes a smartass for a daughter. What's going on here?

POLLY. Nothing's going on. Can't I stay?

EVY. Tonight? You know you can.

POLLY. Okay. I'm staying tonight. (*Starts for bedroom again.*)

EVY. With all that? You must be some heavy sleeper.

POLLY. Okay, *two* nights, let's not haggle.

EVY. Hey, hey, just a minute. Put the suitcase down. (POLLY *looks at her. She puts it down.*) . . . Now look at me.

POLLY. I'm looking.

EVY. And I know what you're thinking. Oh, no, you don't.

POLLY. Why not?

EVY. Because I don't need any roommates, thank you. . . . If you had a beard, it would be different.

POLLY. I don't want to be your roommate, I just want to live with you.

EVY. You lonely? I'll send you to camp. You have a home, what are you bothering me for?

POLLY. You can't throw me out, I'm your flesh and blood.

EVY. I just got rid of my flesh, I'm not sentimental.

POLLY. I've already decided I'm moving in, you have nothing to say about it.

EVY. In the first place, idiot, you're not allowed to live here. It's not up to you or me.

POLLY. And in the second place?

EVY. I don't need a second place. The first one wiped us out. You live where your father tells you to live.

POLLY. Exactly. Where do I put the suitcase?

EVY. Are you telling me *your* father gave you permission to move in here with me?

POLLY. Right.

EVY. *Your* father?

POLLY. That's the one.

EVY. A tall man, grayish hair, wears blue suits, spits a little when he talks?

POLLY. Would you like to speak to him yourself?

EVY. Not sober, I don't. What does your stepmother think about this? What's her name, Lucretia?

POLLY. Felicia.

EVY. Felicia, some name. He must spit pretty good

when he says that. Did she ever get that clicking in her teeth fixed?

POLLY. Nope. Still clicking.

EVY. That's a nice way to live, with a spitter and a clicker. Thank God he didn't get custody of me too.

POLLY. That's why I'm begging you to take me in. I can't do my homework with all that noise.

EVY. God's truth, Polly? He really said yes?

POLLY. He likes me. He wouldn't kid around with my life.

EVY. Why don't I believe it?

POLLY. We've been talking about it for months. He knows how hard you've been trying, he spoke to your doctor, he knows you're alright. . . . And he thinks that you need me now.

EVY. *Now* I need you? Where does he think I've been the last seven years, Guatemala?

POLLY. He knows where you've been.

EVY. And what about you? Is this what you really want?

POLLY. I've been packed for three years. Every June I put in bigger sizes.

EVY. You wanna hear something? My whole body is shaking. I'm scared stiff. I wouldn't know the first thing about taking care of you.

POLLY. I'm seventeen years old. How hard could it be?

EVY. I'll level with you, it's not the best thing I do. I was feeling very motherly one time, I bought a couple of turtles, two for eighty-five cents, Irving and Sam. I fed them once, in the morning they were floating on their backs. I don't think I could go through that again.

POLLY. I'm a terrific swimmer.

EVY. Jesus, the one thing I hoped I wouldn't have is a dumb daughter. What kind of influence would I be on you? I talk filthy. I have always talked filthy. I'm a congenital filthy talker.

POLLY. Son of a bitch.

EVY. I don't think that's funny.

POLLY. Well, I just got here, give me a chance.

EVY. What the hell is the big attraction? I thought we were doing fine with visiting days.

POLLY. When I was nine years old, do you remember what you gave me for Christmas?

EVY. An empty bottle of Dewars White Label? I don't know, I can't remember yesterday.

POLLY. Don't you remember the Gingerbread House with the little gingerbread lady in the window?

EVY. If you say so.

POLLY. I always kept it to remind me of you. Of course today I have the biggest box of crumbs in the neighborhood. Come on, be a sport. Buy me another one this Christmas.

EVY. I don't know if I could afford it.

POLLY. What are you afraid of?

EVY. Of leaving you with the crumbs again. . . . You know what I'm like.

POLLY. I've seen you drunk. Mostly I hated it but one or twice you sure were cute.

EVY. You only saw dress rehearsals. I was very careful around you. A mother doesn't like to get too pissed around her own daughter. Am I supposed to say things like that in front of you? Pissed?

POLLY. If you can do it, you can say it.

EVY. There are other things I can't tell you. . . . Ah, Christ, I might as well tell you. You knew about Lou Tanner.

POLLY. I met him here a few times.

EVY. Did you know we lived here together for eight months?

POLLY. I didn't think he got off a bus in those pajamas.

EVY. Jesus, at least have the decency to be shocked.

POLLY. There's a sixteen-year-old girl who just left school because she's pregnant. You're 43. If you're not allowed, who is?

EVY. How'd I suddenly end up with the Mother of the Year Award?

POLLY. I don't want to judge you, Evy. I just want to live with you.

EVY. You're seventeen years old, it's time you judged me. I just don't want you to get the idea that a hundred and eighty-three pounds of pure alcohol is something called Happy Fat. . . . Many a night I would have thrown myself out that window if I could have squeezed through. . . . I'm not what you'd call an emotionally stable person. You know how many times I was *really* in love since your father and I broke up? I met the only man who ever really meant anything to me about seven maybe eight times. Mr. Right I meet at least twice a week. . . . I sure know true love when I see it. It's wherever I happen to look.

POLLY. You don't have to tell me any of this.

EVY. *I do*, dammit. . . . I want you to know everything, Polly, before you make up your mind. I lived here with that guitar player for eight of the happiest months of my life. Well, why not? He was handsome, funny, ten years younger than me, what more could a woman want? . . . He sat in that chair all day working and writing and I fed him and clothed him and loved him for eight incredible months. . . . And then that dirty bastard— I'm sorry, I'm going to try not to do that anymore.

POLLY. Good.

EVY. No, the hell with it. That dirty bastard. He walked out on me in the middle of the night for an eighteen-year-old Indian hippie. "Princess-Screw-the-Other-Woman." . . . Wait'll she gets old and starts looking like the face on the nickel. And he doesn't have a penny, not a cent. Well, her moccasins'll wear out, we'll see how long that affair lasts. . . . But I sat at that window for six weeks waiting and hoping while I ran through two liquor stores in this neighborhood alone. . . . Finally Toby came in one day and found me face down in the bathtub. . . . I woke up in a sanitarium in Long Island, and the rest isn't very interesting unless you like stories about human torture. . . . But I went through it and I'm here. And I figure, pussycat, that I have only one more chance at this human being business . . . and if I blow it this time, they'll probably bury me in some distillery in Kentucky. . . . And if this is the kind of person you'd like to live with, God has cursed me with one of the all-time great schmucks for a daughter.

POLLY. (*Smiles.*) How'd you like to come and speak at my school?

EVY. (*Adores her for this.*) I think I would rather have you than a mink coat that fits. (*Hugs* POLLY.) You still want to take a shot at it?

POLLY. After that story, I'd pay for a seat.

EVY. Oh, no. If you move in, it's a whole new ball game. If you're going to live here with me, we turn this place into "Little Women." Clean sheets, doilies on the furniture, *TV Guide*, a regular American family.

POLLY. And we can go to church on Sunday. By the way, what religion are we?

EVY. I'll look it up. I've got it here somewhere. . . . I'm going to get a job. Not in show business, a real job. (*Starts pacing.*)

POLLY. I get home from school at four, I could start dinners.

EVY. Can you cook?

POLLY. No, but I can get them started.

EVY. Is that all you can do?

POLLY. I can ride a horse.

EVY. That's it. When we're starving to death, you're the one who rides for help.

POLLY. Can I unpack now?

EVY. Yes, you can unpack now! . . . Holy Christ, Polly, I am suddenly so excited. How did I get so lucky?

POLLY. (*Shrugs.*) Some people have it all. (*Starts into bedroom with suitcase.*)

EVY. See what looks good in the kitchen, I'll put your things away. (*Starts for bedroom as* POLLY *starts for kitchen. They pass on the way.*)

POLLY. So far we're doing terrific.

(EVY *disappears into bedroom.* POLLY *is in the kitchen. Both are Offstage.*)

EVY. (*Offstage.*) What the hell do you have in here, Yankee Stadium?

POLLY. (*Offstage.*) It's my record collection.

(*The FRONT DOORBELL RINGS.*)

EVY. (*Offstage.*) I see a lot of panties here but I don't see any bras. Don't you wear a bra?

POLLY. (*Offstage.*) No. Am I missing a big thrill? (*Comes out of kitchen. Looks toward bedroom but apparently* EVY *hasn't heard it. She crosses and opens door.* LOU TANNER *stands there. He is in his mid-thirties, with scruffy, unmanageable hair, a full, bushy mustache, a dirty turtleneck sweater and light-tan desert boots, very worn. He is, despite his appearance, attractive.* POLLY *is shaken by his ill-timed arrival.*)

POLLY. Hello, Lou!

LOU. (*Looks at her, then past her into the room.*) Hello, Polly.

EVY. (*Offstage.*) I'm not going to ask you what these pills are for because I don't want to know and I don't want to hear.

LOU. She alright?

POLLY. (*Still shaken.*) What? . . . Yes. She's fine.

LOU. Can I come in?

POLLY. (*Looks toward bedroom worriedly.*) Yes, sure. (*He steps into the room. She closes the door behind him.*) How are you?

LOU. I thought she'd be alone. . . . Maybe I ought to come back later.

POLLY. No. No, I'm sure she'll want to see you. (*Calls out.*) Mother! . . . Someone's here.

(LOU *stares at the bedroom door as* POLLY *eyes him nervously. . . .* EVY *appears at the bedroom doorway.*

She has probably recognized Lou's *voice. She comes out of bedroom and faces* Lou.)

Lou. Hello, Evy.

Evy. (*Trying to be cool.*) Hello, Lou. . . . (*A moment of awkward silence.*)

Lou. You look fabulous.

Evy. Thank you.

Lou. How'd you lose so much weight?

Evy. Sheer happiness.

Polly. (*This is no place for her.*) I'll finish unpacking. I'll see you, Lou.

Evy. That's alright, you can stay.

Polly. I'd rather not, if you don't mind. (*Nods at* Lou.) Lou. (*Exits quickly into bedroom.* Evy *and* Lou *stand there eyeing each other.*)

Lou. I checked the hospital, they told me you were coming home today. Rough scene, heh?

Evy. No, I loved it. They showed movies Saturday nights. . . . How's Pocahontas?

Lou. We split about a month ago.

Evy. Ah, that's too bad. What was the problem, couldn't she make it rain?

Lou. She couldn't make it, period. A lot of sexual hangups among the Cherokees. (*Looks around.*) You gonna offer me a cigarette?

Evy. No, but you're welcome to take a bath. You look like the second week of the garbage strike. You living indoors somewhere?

Lou. Eddie Valendo's on the road, I'm using his place.

Evy. I hope he left you food, you look a little shaky.

Lou. Musicians don't eat, Evy, you know that. We live on "soul."

Evy. Whose?

Lou. I wouldn't turn down a bottle of cold beer.

Evy. You asking or begging?

Lou. Is that what you want to hear? Okay, I'm begging.

Evy. I always knew you'd make it big someday. (*Hands him cigarette.*) Here. There's one left. Smoke it when you're older.

Lou. (*Tries to grab her.*) That's my Evy.

Evy. (*Pulling away.*) You are one priceless, unbelievable bastard. You had to walk in here today, didn't you? You had to time it so you'd get me holding my nerves together with spit and coffee.

Lou. What'd you want me to do, phone you from a pay station in Walgreen's? "Hi, Evy, guess who this is?"

Evy. The only thing stopping you was the dime.

Lou. Come on, Evy, I walked seventeen blocks in borrowed shoes. Talk nice to me.

Evy. Like nothing ever happened, right?

Lou. No, it happened. We'll talk about it. But it's hard when you don't look at me. I get the feeling I'm suddenly left all alone in this room.

Evy. (*Turns and looks at him.*) I know the feeling well.

Lou. I'll say one thing for the Indians: Generally speaking, they're not a vindictive people.

Evy. Really, Lou? What'd she do when you walked out on her? Ride into the sunset? Do a little sun dance? Wriggle and bounce her firm little body? You want to tell me about her tight little eighteen-year-old body, Lou?

Lou. Not particularly.

Evy. Come on. Lay it on me. Talk that hip, colorful language you dig so much. Tell me your problems, Lou, you'll get a lot of sympathy from me.

Lou. No problems, Ev. Nothing that can't be worked out.

Evy. Lou, I'm 43 years old and I'm trying to be a grown-up lady. The doctors told me I'm not allowed to drink anymore or have affairs with 33-year-old guitar players. . . . I thank you for this visit. Now go home, find someone your own age and light up some Astro-Turf or whatever you're smoking these days.

Lou. (*Smiles.*) If nothing else, Evy, you have a way

with a phrase. I used to quote you. Word for word. Of course this dumb little Indian chick never saw the humor. We communicated in other ways. But whenever I needed a good honest laugh, I had to quote you, Ev. You weren't in the room, but you were there, you know what I mean?

Evy. It's an image I think I'll cherish forever. . . . Listen, Polly is here and I think we ought to cut this short.

Lou. I want to come back, Ev. (*There is a pause.*) . . . Today, tomorrow, next week . . . but I want to come back.

Evy. I see! . . . Would that be with or without meals?

Lou. Maybe with a little humility. I'll scrape up whatever I can.

Evy. I don't want you to steal just for me.

Lou. There it is, Ev. That's what I've come back for. A little stimulation.

Evy. Try a vibrator.

Lou. Try letting up for two minutes. Take an interest, Ev, ask me how my work is coming.

Evy. How's your work coming, Lou?

Lou. Gee, it's nice of you to take an interest. I'm writing. I'm not selling anything, but I'm writing.

Evy. (*Without emotion.*) I am *enormously* pleased for you.

Lou. You don't give a crap, do you? You never did give a good Goddamn.

Evy. That's too hysterical to be answered.

Lou. Oh, you cared about *me*. I never questioned that. Affection, love, passion, you had it by the tonnage. All I had to do was look at you with anything less than indifference and you were ready to jump in the sack with your shoes on.

Evy. Forgive me. Frigidity is not one of my major hang-ups.

Lou. I could have been a counterman at Riker's, it wouldn't have made any difference to you.

Evy. *Nothing* made any difference to me except you.

Lou. You didn't give a damn if the stuff I wrote was good or not as long as it was finished. "It's terrific, Lou, now come to bed."

Evy. You wrote it, you played it, I listened to it. Short of publishing it there wasn't a hell of a lot more I could do.

Lou. You never really liked it, did you? You never thought I had any real talent, did you?

Evy. I loved it. Everything you wrote I loved.

Lou. Bullshit.

Evy. That's a better way of putting it.

Lou. Then why the hell didn't you say so?

Evy. I had enough trouble getting affection from you without giving you bad reviews.

Lou. I can't believe it. You hated everything I wrote and you never said a word to me until now.

Evy. I'm sorry your ego is hurt posthumously. Alright, I think you're very promising. I'll take a page ad in *Variety*. Now leave me alone.

Lou. You know, Evy, you are the biggest ball-breaking insufferable pain in the ass woman I ever met . . . and I'm standing here enjoying it. . . . I'm cut up and bleeding from abuse and humiliation but at least I know I'm in the room with a living human being . . . (*Softening.*) I haven't had a good all-out fight like that in three months. . . . I have also, in that time, not put down a piece of music worth the price of the paper. . . . Maybe you're right. At best I'm mediocre. But mediocre is better than wasting good music sheets. . . . Come on, Evy. The truth is, while I was here, I functioned. And when I functioned, you functioned.

Evy. Evy and Lou functioning, one of the great love stories of all time.

Lou. (*With some humor.*) Well, maybe not the greatest, just the most original. . . . What do you say, Ev? Make a contribution to the world of serious music.

Evy. I already gave.

Lou. Christ, Evy, you want me to say it, I'll say it. I need you very badly.

Evy. For how long, Lou? Until you run off with the Chinese hat check girl at Trader Vic's?

Lou. Evy, I swear—

Evy. Don't make me any promises. I just left a hospital filled with people waiting for promises.

Lou. Come on for crise sakes, you had that problem for twenty years before you ever met me.

Evy. No argument. I just don't want it for twenty years after.

Lou. What are you going to tell me, you're cured? You had buttermilk for twelve weeks and now you'll live happily ever after? . . . There's still a whole life to get through, Evy. . . . I'm not coming in here offering you any phoney promises. Sure, in six weeks I may find another cute-assed little chick, and in eight weeks they might find you under the piano with a case of Thunderbird wine. Then again, maybe not. Together, Evy, we don't add up to one strong person. I just think together we have a better chance.

Evy. What I need now is a relative, not a relationship. And I have one in there unpacking.

Lou. Who are you kidding?

Evy. She'll be here in the morning. That's good enough for me.

Lou. The mornings have never been your problem.

Evy. We were just going to have dinner. I'd ask you to stay but it's just the immediate family.

Lou. Well, it was kind of a slow afternoon, I just thought I'd ask. . . . I'm really glad to see you in good shape, Ev. . . . Take care of yourself.

Evy. That's the general idea.

Lou. (*At the door.*) You still have ten seconds to change your mind. (*Waits. No reply.*) My, how time flies. (*Opens door, about to go.*)

Evy. Lou! (*He stops, turns.*) . . . Will you call me sometime? Just to say hello?

LOU. (*Looks at her.*) Probably not. (*Turns, goes, closes door behind him. Evy stands there a moment. . . . The bedroom door opens, POLLY comes out.*)

POLLY. I didn't hear a word . . . But can I say something?

EVY. Only if it'll make me laugh. . . . Are you unpacked yet?

POLLY. It would take me two minutes to put it all back.

EVY. If you're unpacked, then wash your hands, set the table and light the stove. It's dinnertime.

POLLY. (*Brightly.*) Okay, Evy.

EVY. And none of that Evy crap. . . . I'm your mother. I want a little respect, for crise sakes! (*Starts to remove tablecloth from table as POLLY, beaming, exits into kitchen.*)

CURTAIN

ACT TWO

SCENE: *Three weeks later. About nine o'clock at night.*

AT RISE: POLLY *is on phone.*

POLLY. (*Into phone.*) Hello? . . . Is this Joe Allen's Bar? . . . Could you tell me if Evelyn Meara is there, please? . . . *Evy* Meara, that's right. . . . I see. . . . Was she there at all today? . . .

(*The front door opens, unseen by* POLLY. EVY *enters carrying a Saks Fifth Avenue shopping bag.*)

EVY. I'm here, I'm here. Just what I need, a trusting daughter. (*Closes the door.*)
POLLY. (*Into phone.*) Never mind. Thank you. (*Hangs up. Turns to* EVY.)
EVY. (*Puts down the packages.*) If you knew what a terrific day I had you wouldn't be worrying about me. . . . I've got sensational news. . . . I was picked up today. . . . He was eighty-six years old with a cane and a limp, but he really dug me. I don't think he could see me or hear me too good but we really hit it off. . . . If I don't get any better offers this week, I'm going to contact him at the Home. Hello, pussycat, give your mother a kiss. (*Kisses* POLLY *on the cheek, who receives it coldly.*) What's wrong?
POLLY. It's almost nine o'clock.
EVY. You're kidding?
POLLY. (*Points to clock on mantel.*) I'm not kidding. It's almost nine o'clock.
EVY. Alright, don't get excited. What did I miss, the eclipse, what happened?

37

POLLY. You don't call, you don't leave a note, you don't tell me where you're going to be. I'm expecting you home for dinner at six-thirty and you don't show and I'm scared to death. What happened? Where were you?

EVY. Hanging around the men's room in the subway. . . . I had a good day. You want to hear the details or you want to yell at me?

POLLY. I want to yell at you.

EVY. You can't yell at me, I'm your mother. I missed your dinner. Oh, God, Polly, I'm sorry. What did you make?

POLLY. I don't know. Something out of the cookbook. It was brown and it was hot. . . . If you want some, it's in the kitchen now. It's yellow and it's cold.

EVY. (*Hugging her.*) Don't be mad at me. All I've got in the world is you and that eighty-six-year-old gimp, don't be mad at me. Let me tell you what happened today.

POLLY. Did you eat?

EVY. Yes, I think so. . . . Listen to what happened. I ran into this old girl friend of mine who used to work in the clubs—

POLLY. What do you mean you think so? Don't you know if you ate or not?

EVY. I ate, I ate! I had a sandwich for lunch. I'll run up to Lenox Hill and take an X ray for you. . . . Will you listen to my story?

POLLY. You mean you haven't had anything to eat except lunch?

EVY. It didn't say "Lunch" on the sandwich. Maybe it was a "Dinner" sandwich, I don't know. What are you taking in school this week, nagging? Let me tell you my story.

POLLY. You don't sleep well and I never see you eat, so I'm worried about you.

EVY. Who says I don't sleep well?

POLLY. I watch you at night.

EVY. Then *you're* the one who doesn't sleep well.

POLLY. You're in the living room until five, six in the morning, pacing and smoking and coughing. I hear you in there.

EVY. It's the television. I listen to Cancer commercials.

POLLY. Making phone calls in the middle of the night. . . . Who were you calling at four o'clock in the morning?

EVY. The weather bureau.

POLLY. At four o'clock in the morning?

EVY. I like to know what it's going to be like at five o'clock. . . . Jesus! Two more years of this, you're going to be a professional pain in the ass.

POLLY. Okay, fine with me. If you don't give a crap, I don't give a crap.

EVY. And watch your Goddamned language.

POLLY. If you don't watch yours, why should I watch mine?

EVY. I talk this way. It's an impediment. You want me to wear braces on my mouth?

POLLY. You might as well. You never *eat* anything except a cup of coffee for breakfast.

EVY. What the hell difference does it make?

POLLY. Because if you don't take care of your body, it's not going to take care of you.

EVY. I don't want to take care of my body. I want somebody else to take care of it. Why do you think I'm talking to eighty-year-old men?

POLLY. You're infuriating. It's like talking to a child.

EVY. (*Turns away.*) I don't get any respect. How the hell am I going to be a mother if I don't get any respect?

POLLY. How am I going to respect you when you don't respect yourself?

EVY. (*Looks up in despair.*) Oh, Christ, I'm a flop mother. Three weeks and I blew it. Don't be angry, Polly. Don't be mad at me.

POLLY. And stop apologizing. You're my mother. Make *me* apologize to you for talking the way I did.

EVY. It won't happen again, sweetheart, I promise.

POLLY. (*Vehemently.*) Don't promise *me,* promise yourself! I can't live my life *and* yours. *You've* got to take over, *you've* got to be the one in charge around here.

EVY. Listen, you're really getting me crazy now. Why don't you write all the rules and regulations nice and neat on a piece of paper and I'll do whatever it says. Put on one page where I yell at you and one page where you yell at me. . . . Now you want to hear what happened to me this afternoon or not?

POLLY. (*It's hard not to like* EVY. POLLY *smiles at her.*) What happened this afternoon?

EVY. I think I have a job.

POLLY. You're kidding? Where?

EVY. Well . . . (*Pacing.*) I was in Gucci's looking for a birthday present for Toby . . . when suddenly I meet this old girl friend of mine who used to be a vocalist in this singing group. . . . Four Macks and a Truck or some Goddamned thing. . . . Anyway, she can't get over my gorgeous new figure and asks what I'm doing lately and I tell her, I'm looking for good, honest work, preferably around a lot of single men, like an aircraft carrier, Okinawa, something like that. . . . You're looking at me funny. If you're thinking of heating up the cold, yellow stuff, forget it.

POLLY. I'm just listening.

EVY. Alright. . . . Well, she starts to tell me how she's out of the business now and is married to an Italian with four restaurants on Long Island and right away I dig he's in with the mob. I mean one restaurant, you're in business, four restaurants it's the Mafia. . . . Anyway, he's got a place in Garden City and he's looking for an attractive hostess who says, "Good evening, right this way please," and wriggles her behind and gets a hundred and ninety bucks a week. . . . So I played it very cool, and nonchalantly got down on my knees, kissed her shoes, licked her ankles and carried her packages out the store.

POLLY. A hostess in a restaurant? Is that what you want to do?

EVY. No, what I *want* to do is be a masseur at the New York Athletic Club, but there are no openings. . . . Can I finish my story?

POLLY. Why don't you finish your story?

EVY. Thank you, I'll finish my story. . . . So we go around the corner to Schrafft's and she buys me a sherry and we sit there chatting like a couple of Scarsdale debutantes—me, the former lush, and her, a chippie married to Joe Bananas . . . and she writes down the address and I have to be— (*Consults scrap of paper in her pocket.*) at the Blue Cockatoo Restaurant in Garden City at ten o'clock tomorrow morning where Lucky Luciano's nephew will interview me. All this in one day, *plus* getting my knees rubbed by an eighty-six-year-old degenerate on the crosstown bus. . . . And you're going to sit there and tell me there's no God. . . . (*Looks at* POLLY *expectantly, hoping* POLLY *will be as exuberant and enthusiastic about her prospects as she is. But* POLLY *just glares at her.*) What's the matter?

POLLY. You had a glass of sherry?

EVY. (*Turns away.*) Oh, Christ.

POLLY. Why did you have a glass of sherry?

EVY. Because the waitress put it down in front of me.

POLLY. They don't put it down in front of you unless you order it. I don't understand you.

EVY. I don't understand *you!* I rush home happy, excited, bubbling with good news and who do I find when I get here, a seventeen-year-old cop! I am not loaded, I am not smashed, I am thrilled to death because I spent a whole day out of this house and I came home alive and noticed and even wanted.

POLLY. Do you need a drink to feel that?

EVY. I was tense, I was afraid of blowing the job. So I had one stinking little drink. Did you ever have a cocktail in Schrafft's? Half of it is painted on the glass.

POLLY. That isn't the point. You could have had coffee or tea or milk.

EVY. Thank you, miss, when do we land in Chicago? . . . I don't want to talk about it anymore. Go inside and study. When you pass French, we'll discuss it in a foreign language. Until then, shape up or ship out or whatever the hell that expression is.

POLLY. . . . No, listen, (*Looks at her quietly a moment.*) I think it's terrific.

EVY. You think what's terrific?

POLLY. About today, about getting the job. I really do. When will you start?

EVY. Well, in the first place, I didn't get it yet. And in the second place, I'm not so sure I'm going to take it.

POLLY. (*Puzzled.*) Then what's all the excitement about?

EVY. . . . About being asked . . . About being wanted.

POLLY. I'm sorry—I don't think I understand.

EVY. (*Crosses to* POLLY, *holds her head in her arms.*) Please God, I hope you never do. . . . (*Smiles at her, trying to be more cheerful.*) Listen, how about one more chance at being a mother? If I screw up, you can buy out my contract for a hundred dollars and I'll move out.

POLLY. (*Takes* EVY's *hand.*) Who's going to bring me up?

EVY. (*Shrugs.*) I'll set you on automatic. . . . (*Crosses back to shopping bag.*) Hey, come on, get dressed. We have a party that started fifteen minutes ago.

POLLY. What party?

EVY. Toby's birthday. (*Takes out present from shopping bag.*) She's forty years old today. She's promised to take off her makeup and reveal her true identity.

POLLY. I've got to study. I have a science test on Monday.

EVY. Flunk it! Men don't like you if you're too smart. (*Takes out bottle of champagne. She looks at* POLLY *who stares at her meaningfully.*) I'm pouring! That's all I'm doing is pouring.

POLLY. Who's coming?

EVY. Jimmy, Marty and Toby. (*Starts to cross to kitchen with champagne bottle,* POLLY *starts for bedroom.*)

POLLY. What should I wear? How about the blue chiffon?

EVY. You can wear black crepe as long as your boobs don't bounce around. (*Crosses toward kitchen.*)

POLLY. (*At bedroom door.*) Mother?

EVY. Yes?

POLLY. Don't take that job. You're too good for it. Hold out for something better.

EVY. I'm so glad you said that. Who the Christ even knows where Garden City is? . . . Hey, let's have a good time tonight. I'm beginning to feel like my old self again.

POLLY. Hey, listen, I forgot to tell you. We have a lunch date tomorrow.

EVY. (*In kitchen. Busy with bottles.*) Who has a lunch date?

POLLY. We do. You, me and Daddy.

EVY. (*Stops what she's doing and comes out to kitchen doorway. Dismayed.*) *What* Daddy?

POLLY. *My* Daddy. You remember, Felicia's husband? . . . 12 o'clock at Rumplemayer's.

EVY. Why didn't you tell me?

POLLY. Because I never see you. *Now* I see you. He just wants to have lunch with us, talk, see how we're getting along.

EVY. We're getting along fine.

POLLY. He knows. He just wants to see.

EVY. You mean he's checking to see what shape I'm in? Christ, he's gonna look in my ears, under my fingernails, I'll never pass.

POLLY. He just wants to talk.

EVY. Is he gonna ask questions, like what's the capital of Bulgaria?

POLLY. Stop worrying. It'll be alright. I've got to get

dressed, Oh, and if he does, the capital is Sofia. (*Goes into bedroom.*)

Evy. (*Standing there a moment.*) Just what I needed. A physical examination in Rumplemayer's. (*Starts into kitchen.*) I should have had *two* sherries today.

(*There is a moment's pause. The DOORBELL RINGS.*)

Polly. Are you getting it?

Evy. (*Comes out of kitchen.*) If I was getting it I wouldn't be looking for jobs all day. . . . Get dressed. (*Crosses to door and opens it.* Jimmy *stands there looking glum and expressionless. He walks past her into the room.* Evy *closes the door.*) No kiss? . . . No hello? . . . Aren't you going to look up, maybe you're in the wrong apartment? (Jimmy *sits without taking off his coat. He chews his thumbnail. His leg begins to shake.*) If you're that hungry, have some nuts. (*He doesn't acknowledge.*) What's the matter? What happened?

Jimmy. (*His leg is still shaking.*) I'm okay, I'm not upset anymore, I'm alright. . . . I know my leg is shaking, but I'm alright.

Evy. Why? What's wrong?

Jimmy. They pushed the opening of the show back one night. . . . It's opening Tuesday instead of Monday.

Evy. Alright, it's Tuesday instead of Monday. What's so terrible?

Jimmy. It's also another actor instead of me. They fired me. The little son of a bitch fired me three nights before the opening.

Evy. Oh, Christ.

Jimmy. Fired by a nineteen-year-old producer from Oklahoma A & M. . . . Look at that leg. Do you realize the tension that must be going on in my body right now?

Evy. Oh, Jimmy, no, don't tell me.

Jimmy. If he didn't like me, why'd he hire me in the

first place, heh? . . . The entire cast is shocked. Shocked, Evy. Three nights before the opening.

EVY. They must be shocked.

JIMMY. He didn't even get somebody else to tell me. He wanted to tell me himself. . . . He stood there with a little smile on his Goddamned baby face and said, "Sorry, Jimmy, it's just not working out." . . . Nineteen years old, can you imagine, Evy? . . . Ten thousand kids a month getting drafted and they leave *this* one behind to produce my show.

EVY. What can I say? What can I do?

JIMMY. Three nights before the opening. My name was in the Sunday *Times* ad. I've got eighteen relatives from Paterson, New Jersey, coming to the opening. Six of them already sent me telegrams. . . . My Aunt Rosario sent me a Candygram, I already ate the Goddamned candy.

EVY. Oh, God, I can't bear it. Tell me what to do for you.

JIMMY. Everybody in the cast wanted to walk out on the show, I wouldn't let them. Even the director was crazy about me. . . . I can't breathe, I can't catch my breath, I'm so upset. . . . I gotta calm down, Evy, I'll be alright.

EVY. I know how you feel. I swear. I know exactly how you feel.

JIMMY. You do? You know how it feels for a grown man to plead and beg to a child, Evy? A *child!* . . . I said to him, "You're not happy, I'll do it any way you want. Faster, slower, louder, I'll wear a dress, I'll shave my head, I'll relieve myself on the stage in front of my own family, I'm an actor, give me a chance to act." . . . He turned his back on me and shoved a Tootsie Roll in his mouth.

EVY. Listen, maybe the play won't be a hit. Maybe it'll be a bomb, it'll close in one night, you're lucky you're out of it.

JIMMY. What do you mean, maybe? It's got no chance. It's the worst piece of crap ever put on a stage. That's why I'm so humiliated. To get fired from a piece of

EVY. (*Offstage.*) I have never heard laughs like that in my life.

JIMMY. In my life, I never heard laughs like that. . . . And I don't have to get laughs all the time. My God, the things I've done . . . "Phaedra," "Mother Courage," "Rhinoceros," "The Balcony," "Detective Story" . . . Jesus, remember "Detective Story"? The second hood? I was incredible.

EVY. (*Offstage.*) You were brilliant. (*We hear a cork pop from champagne bottle.*)

JIMMY. When did you see me in "Detective Story"? I did that in Columbus, Ohio.

EVY. (*Comes out with champagne bottle and two glasses.*) You were so brilliant I didn't have to see it. (*Hands* JIMMY *a glass. He takes it without being aware he has it.*)

JIMMY. I played the Dauphin in "St. Joan" at the Cleveland Auditorium three years before that nineteen-year-old rich Oklahoma idiot schmuck was born.

EVY. (*Pours champagne into his glass, then hers.*) Forget it. He's not worth it.

JIMMY. I actually pleaded with him. I humiliated myself in front of the entire cast. I had no shame. No shame, Evy. (*Drinks.*) Opening night my mother will throw herself in front of a rented limousine.

EVY. That's the best thing that could happen to your mother. (*Sips a little more.*)

JIMMY. I don't wish anybody in the world harm. I don't curse anybody. I want everybody to live their lives healthy and without pain . . . but I pray that little bastard gets a Baby Ruth stuck in his throat and chokes him on the spot. (*Drinks more champagne.* Evy *pours more into his glass. He suddenly watches her and realizes what's happening.*) . . . Oh, my God, what am I doing? I'm sitting here drinking with you. Are you crazy? Are you out of your mind? Put that glass down. (*Reaches for it but she pulls it away.*)

EVY. I'm not drinking, I'm sipping.

JIMMY. You've already sipped a whole glass. Give it to me.

EVY. You think I'm going to stand here and watch you have a breakdown on ginger ale? I need help too.

JIMMY. You put your lips to that glass one more time, you're going to need more than help.

EVY. (*Holds glass up.*) Alright, I'm through, I'm through. (*Then she raises glass to lips and finishes it.*) There! Alright?

JIMMY. Why do you do that to me? Didn't I have enough heartache today?

EVY. A grown man is crying, you want me to sit down and read *Newsweek?* I'm sorry, I panicked.

JIMMY. You didn't panic, you drank. Panicking is when you scream and run around like a lunatic.

EVY. I will. I promise. Next time I'll panic. Better still, don't tell me your problems. You got a twelve-year-old niece, tell her your troubles, kids love to cry.

JIMMY. (*Turns away from her.*) I'm standing there drinking with her. I see the glass in her hand and I'm drinking with her.

EVY. (*Walks around in front of him to get his attention.*) Don't be mad at me. Everybody's mad at me today. Show me a little tenderness, I'll show you a terrific person.

JIMMY. (*Looks at her . . . wilts.*) How could I be mad at you? You loved me in "Detective Story" and never even saw it. (*Hugs her. The DOORBELL RINGS.*)

EVY. (*Low.*) Don't tell Polly. Don't tell her I drank, tell her I panicked.

JIMMY. Some mood I'm in for a party. Christ!

EVY. (*Calls out.*) Hey, Pol, come on, they're here.

POLLY. (*Offstage.*) I don't know how to work the brassiere.

EVY. (*At the door. To* JIMMY.) Try and be happy tonight. You won't have to do it for another year. (*JIMMY nods cheerlessly at her. She opens the door.* TOBY *stands there, looking absolutely ravishing in a new dress. She smiles at* EVY.) Oh, God, that's a pretty woman. Look, Jimmy. Look at the pretty woman.

JIMMY. (*Smiles.*) Oh, yes. That's a pretty woman.

EVY. (*To* JIMMY.) Go, sweetheart. Go kiss the pretty woman.

(JIMMY *crosses in front of* EVY *and kisses* TOBY *on the cheek.*)

JIMMY. Happy birthday, darling.

TOBY. (*Smiles.*) Thank you. (*Speaks softly.* EVY *crosses to* TOBY.)

EVY. Happy birthday, pretty woman. (*Hugs* TOBY.)

TOBY. Thank you, Evelyn. (*Crosses to sofa and sits, opening her purse.*)

EVY. (*Looks toward hall outside.*) Isn't Marty with you?

TOBY. No. (JIMMY *closes the door.*)

EVY. . . . Is he coming later?

TOBY. (*Busy powdering.*) I don't think so.

EVY. (*Looks at* JIMMY, *then at* TOBY.) You don't *think* so? Don't you know?

TOBY. Yes, I know. He's not coming later. (*Looks around.*) Isn't Polly here?

EVY. He's not coming for your birthday party? . . . Are you going to tell me he's *working* tonight?

TOBY. No, he's not working. He just couldn't come. To my birthday party. (*Takes out compact and begins to powder her already highly powdered face.*)

EVY. Why not?

TOBY. . . . Well, I didn't catch everything he said . . . because he was very busy packing . . . but it seems that Martin wants a divorce. (*Smiles at them as though she told them nothing more startling than it's raining outside. . . .* JIMMY *and* EVY *stare at her, stunned.* TOBY *suddenly controls the flood of tears that are threatening to come by putting her hand to her eye, but we do hear a faint sigh from her.*) . . . Is there anything to eat in the refrigerator? (*Gets up and quickly crosses into the kitchen to release the floodgates.*)

JIMMY. (*Looks up to heaven, clasping hands.*) Oh, sweet Mother of Jesus! You just going to stand there? Say something to her! Do something! (*But EVY stands there.*) Toby! Toby! (*Runs off to kitchen after TOBY. EVY turns, looks around, sees that no one is looking and quickly pours her off a glass of champagne. She drinks it quickly, then puts glass down. POLLY emerges from the bedroom, looking lovely and feminine.*)

POLLY. (*Arms extended.*) Happy birthday! (*Looks around.*) Where's the birthday lady?

EVY. (*Motions toward the kitchen.*) With the great American actor.

POLLY. Do I look alright?

EVY. (*Despondent.*) Don't count on applause.

JIMMY. (*Comes out of the kitchen.*) She's alright. Give her a couple of seconds. (*To POLLY.*) Hello, Angel. Don't you look gorgeous.

POLLY. (*Beaming.*) I was thinking of wearing this for your opening. Okay? (JIMMY *looks at* EVY, *then crosses away.* POLLY *looks at them, then to* EVY.) I detect tenseness. Is there tenseness at this party?

EVY. And it's only ten after nine.

TOBY. (*Comes out of the kitchen. She seems composed.*) I love the cake, Evy. It's a beautiful cake. . . . Oh, Polly, how sweet. How sweet and beautiful you are. I was the same way.

POLLY. (*Crosses to her.*) Happy birthday, Toby. (*They kiss.*)

TOBY. Thank you, darling. It's so good to see you. I never see you. I was so anxious to see you tonight and spend some time with you. I never spend enough time with you. Would you excuse us, darling, I have to talk to your mother.

POLLY. (*Puzzled.*) Now?

EVY. Now.

POLLY. (*Shrugs.*) I'll study French. Call me when the games begin. (*Exits into bedroom.*)

TOBY. She's going to be beautiful, Evy. There is nothing so important in a woman's life as being beautiful. . . . (*There is a pause. No one says anything.*) . . . Anyone want to hear about my divorce?

JIMMY. You're not serious. You had a fight. That's all it was, a little fight, right?

TOBY. No, there's going to be an actual divorce. He is, at the very moment we're speaking, getting advice from his brother, the lawyer, and sympathy from his understanding sister-in-law who happens to know a great deal about sympathy because of those two huge warts on the side of her nose. . . . I'm fine. I'm perfectly fine. Really.

EVY. What happened tonight? Don't describe what you were wearing, just the details.

TOBY. There are no details. He wants a divorce, it's that simple. . . . Do you have any canapes, darling? I think I forgot to eat in all the excitement.

EVY. You caught him at the Americana Hotel with a stewardess from Delta Airlines, right?

TOBY. It wouldn't bother me if I caught him at his brother's house with his sister-in-law. . . . Or his sister's house with his brother-in-law. . . . It's not another woman.

JIMMY. Then what is it?

TOBY. . . . I must have something to drink.

EVY. (*To* JIMMY.) The ladies need a drink.

JIMMY. (*Quickly.*) *I'll* get it. (*Moves hurriedly and gets the champagne bottle from where* EVY *left it and pours a glass for* TOBY.)

TOBY. (*Takes a deep breath.*) Martin—has grown accustomed to my face. (*She is visibly wounded but is trying hard not to show the hurt.*) . . . Accustomed to my touch, accustomed to my voice . . . and I think he's a little bored with my hair. (*Looks at them, forces a smile, sips a little wine.*) . . . He's devoted to me. . . . He is respectful of me. . . . He is indebted to me . . . but he's having a lot of trouble sleeping with me. For some inexplicable reason . . . "inexplicable" is his word . . . he has had no desire to make sexual advances towards me. . . . He makes them, but there's no desire. . . . It's as though someone were in back of him "pushing." . . . He is not tired . . . he is not overworked . . . he is not distracted. . . . He is simply—"turned off." That's *my* word.

JIMMY. (*About to say something helpful.*) Toby, for God's sakes—

TOBY. Did you know . . . that in 1950 I was voted the prettiest girl at the University of Michigan? . . . An All-American halfback was willing to give up a trip to the Rose Bowl for one night of my favors. . . . In 1951 I switched schools and was voted the prettiest girl at the University of Southern California. . . . I received on the average of fifteen sexual proposals a week . . . at least two from the faculty. . . .

EVY. Alright, Toby. . . .

TOBY. When I was sixteen I was offered a seven-year contract by R.K.O. Pictures. They knew I couldn't act, they didn't even care. They said the way I looked, it wasn't important. . . . When I was seventeen years old, a married psychiatrist in Los Angeles drove his car into a tree because I wouldn't answer his phone calls. You can read all of this in my diaries, I still have them.

EVY. Toby, please stop.

TOBY. When I was nineteen I had an affair with a boy who was the son of the largest book publisher in the world. . . . When I was twenty, I had an affair *with* the largest book publisher in the world. . . . The son threatened to kill the father but by then I was having an affair with the youngest symphony conductor in the world.

EVY. Jimmy, for God's sakes, will you say something to her?

TOBY. (*Accelerating.*) When I was twenty-three, I *slept* with a member of the British Royal Household. I slept with him. In the British Royal House. . . . There is a senator living in Washington, D.C., today, who will vote any way I want him to vote by spending just one morning in Washington, D.C. . . . I have had more men, men in politics, in the arts, in the sciences, more of the most influential men in the world, in love with me, desirous of me, *hungry* for me, than any woman I ever met in my entire life . . . and that son-of-a-bitch four-hundred-dollar-a-week television salesman tells me *he isn't interested??* . . . *Then let him get out, I don't need him!! (And she begins to sob uncontrollably.)* Evy . . . Evy . . . !

Evy. *(Is distraught, of course, with her own inability to help. Paces.)* Jimmy, do something or I'll kill myself.

Jimmy. *(Quickly crosses to* Toby *and sits on arm of chair, putting his arm around her to comfort her.)* It's alright, Toby, it's alright.

Toby. *(Looks up at* Jimmy.) I am still beautiful and I am still desirable, I don't care how old I am.

Jimmy. Of course you are, my God! . . . Evy, give her some more wine.

Toby. *(To* Evy.) Evy, no woman has ever taken care of herself the way I have. (Evy *crosses to champagne bottle.)* I am forty years old today and my skin is as smooth and as creamy white as it was when I was sixteen.

Jimmy. Drink this. Come on, Toby, you'll feel better.

Toby. We spent two months on the beach at Westhampton last summer and the sun never once touched my body. . . . I wore more clothes on the beach than I do in New York in January. . . . In Acapulco last year the Mexicans thought I was some kind of a White Goddess. They would bow to me on the streets. Jimmy, remember I told you that story?

Jimmy. I remember that story.

Toby. *(Addressing* Evy *again.)* Last December in Los Angeles, that boy I had an affair with, the book publisher's son, called me at the Beverly Hills Hotel, *dying* to see me. He came over and we had cocktails in the Polo Lounge. . . . He looked like my father. My *father,* Evy.

. . . And then the waiter came over, and I swear, may God strike me dead as I sit here with my dearest friends . . . the waiter asked for my I.D. card. . . . I don't even think it's twenty-one in California, I think you have to be eighteen. . . . I know it's dark in the Polo Lounge, but it's not *that* dark.

JIMMY. (*To* EVY, *as though it would help* TOBY.) It's not, I've been there, I know.

TOBY. (*Sips a little more champagne.*) I'm not a stupid woman, I know that. I've traveled a lot, I'm well-read, well-educated, I went to two universities. . . . I have had marvelous, intellectual conversations with some of the most brilliant men in the world . . . but the things that men admire most in a woman are her femininity and her beauty. . . . That's the truth, Evy, I know it is. (*To* JIMMY.) Isn't that the first thing you men look for in a woman, Jimmy?

JIMMY. (*Hesitates.*) . . . Yes, I suppose it is.

TOBY. (*Back to* EVY.) . . . I know I'm vain, Evy, I never pretended I'm not. I devote my whole day to myself, to my face, to my body. . . . I sleep all morning so my eyes won't be red. . . . I bathe twice a day in soft water, I buy the world's most expensive creams, I have a Japanese man who lives in White Plains come down twice a week just to do my feet. Did you know that, Evy? (EVY *nods.* TOBY *turns to* JIMMY.) Did you?

JIMMY. I didn't know he was Japanese.

TOBY. I swear. He says I have the feet of an Oriental woman. Can you imagine, Evy. Born in Grand Rapids, Michigan, with the feet of an Oriental woman. . . . But I've never done it for me. None of it. . . . It's what Martin wanted when he came into his house at night, what all men want. . . . Femininity and beauty. . . . But, Evy—if it no longer interests Martin . . . then I assure you . . . somewhere soon, someplace, someone else will be very . . . very . . . very . . . interested! (*Her voice has trailed off almost becoming inaudible at the end. There is a long, desperate silence in the room.*)

EVY. (*Finally.*) . . . For purely medicinal purposes, I'm having a drink. (*Starts for bottle.*)

JIMMY. (*Warning.*) Evy!

EVY. I'm only a hundred and thirty pounds, but if you try and stop me, I'll kill you. . . . *One* drink, for Christ's sakes.

JIMMY. You *had* one drink.

EVY. For *your* story. Now I need one for hers. (*Pours into glass.*)

TOBY. (*Looks up as if in the room for the first time.*) What's the matter? What's going on?

EVY. *Nothing's* going on but it's going to start right now. . . . We've *all* had a few minor setbacks, but it's a birthday party . . . and I don't give a shit if the room is on fire, we're going to start having some fun. (*Drinks her glass of champagne quickly, then looks at bottle and holds it up.*) We need a new bottle. (*Calls out.*) Polly! Fun and games.

TOBY. (*Pulling her things together.*) I'm not staying, I just wanted to talk to someone.

EVY. Nobody's leaving this room until we're all happy. Now sit down, dammit. Drink your booze. (*Drinks a little more from her glass. The wine is now beginning to take effect on* EVY. *Being an alcoholic, it doesn't take much wine or time.*) Jesus, what a bunch of depressing people.

POLLY. (*Comes out. Big smile.*) Okay, who do I dance with?

EVY. (*Points to* POLLY.) Now *that's* the kind of person you invite to a party. (*To* POLLY.) So far it's just you and me, kid, but we're gonna goose things up. Put on one of your records, I'll get some more wine. (*Starts for kitchen.*) And none of that folk singing crap where they throw babies in the Tallahatchie River, I want some real music, pussycat. (*Goes off into kitchen.*)

POLLY. (*Looks after her.*) Is she alright? What's going on?

JIMMY. Nothing. Everything's fine.

TOBY. I think I must have upset her. Did I upset her, Jimmy?

JIMMY. It's not you, it's everybody. We're all upsetting each other. Some friends. . . .

POLLY. She had a drink at Schrafft's this afternoon, did she tell you?

JIMMY. At Schrafft's? Who the hell goes off the wagon at Schrafft's?

TOBY. I shouldn't have said all that to her. I could see she was very upset. (*They both look worriedly toward* EVY *in the kitchen. . . . A cork explodes in the kitchen.* EVY *comes out with opened bottle of champagne.*)

EVY. Goddamned cheap champagne, I had to make the noise with my tongue. . . . Glasses up, everyone. . . . (*Looks at silent phonograph, then at* POLLY.) You're not going to play that louder, right?

POLLY. (*Going for bottle.*) Let me pour it, Mother.

EVY. Ooh, you hear that? Mother she calls me. If it's one thing I know how to get, it's respect.

TOBY. Evy, don't pay attention to what I said before. Everything's going to be alright, honestly.

EVY. No, listen, you have a major problem. You and Marty are only making it two times a day, if I were you, I'd kill myself. (*Pours wine in* TOBY's *glass.*)

TOBY. (*Embarrassed.*) Evy, please. Can we discuss this later?

EVY. What's the matter? You're worried about Polly? *My* Polly? You don't know about kids today, do you? (*Puts arm around* POLLY.) She could give you a sex lecture right now, your eyebrows would fall out. (*To* POLLY.) Am I right? Is that the truth, Polly? (POLLY *forces a smile and shrugs.*)

JIMMY. May I have the wine, please?

EVY. What do you think, kids learn about sex today the way you and I did? In rumble seats? They have closed circuit television— (*To* POLLY.) —am I right? Actual demonstrations. Two substitute teachers go at it in the gymnasium and the kids take notes. Is that the truth?

POLLY. (*Smiles, embarrassed.*) That's the truth.

EVY. It's the truth. Polly has a sixteen-year-old girl friend in school who got knocked up for homework. Am I lying? Heh?

POLLY. (*Weakly.*) Nope.

EVY. (*Pours some wine in her own glass and drinks it. She laughs.*) Oh, Christ, that's funny. (*No one else laughs.*) Look how funny you all think it is. . . . Gee, what a terrific party. Later on we'll get some fluid and embalm each other. Polly, get a glass, you have to drink to Toby's birthday.

POLLY. (*Reaches for bottle.*) Can I pour it myself?

EVY. (*Holding back bottle.*) What's the matter, you don't trust me? One glass, that's all I'm going to have. . . . My daughter is worried about me. (*Puts arm around* POLLY *again.*) Do you know what it is to have a daughter worried about you? It is the *single greatest* pleasure in the world. . . . In the *world.* . . . (*To* TOBY.) You can have your toes tickled by a Jap, I'll take a daughter worrying about me any time. (*Sips from her glass. Is beginning to lose coordination and control.*) I don't even deserve it. The truth, Polly, I don't deserve it. You grew up, you saw the bus driver more than you saw me, am I right?

JIMMY. Polly, why don't you get the cake?

EVY. No, it's alright, Polly and I understand each other. We have an agreement. She doesn't bug me about the past and I don't bug her about not wearing underwear.

TOBY. Evy, stop, you're embarrassing her.

EVY. I am not. Am I embarrassing you, sweetheart? I'm not embarrassing you, am I?

POLLY. (*Good-naturedly.*) I'll let you embarrass me if you let me take your glass.

EVY. (*Holds glass away from* POLLY *but ignores her remark.*) I told you I'm not embarrassing her. I mean the girl is *beautiful.* Toby, if you saw her sleeping in the raw you'd kill yourself. It's all firm. Remember "firm"? You don't remember firm.

POLLY. (*Forcing smile.*) Okay, *now* I'm getting embarrassed.

EVY. (*Going right on.*) The body of a young woman is God's greatest achievement. . . . Of course, He could have built it to last longer but you can't have everything.

TOBY. Evy, it's my birthday and you're not making me very happy. Let's not have any more wine.

EVY. Why doesn't everybody relax? It's like a Goddamn Telethon for Palsy. Come on, a toast. A toast for my friend Toby. Jimmy, you do it. You're the toastmaster. . . . A toast, everyone.

JIMMY. Evy, I don't think anyone's in the mood.

EVY. Well, *put* 'em in the mood. What else you got to do? You're not working! . . . (*Pulls him reluctantly to the middle of the floor.*)

JIMMY. I'm never good at these things. I never know what to say.

EVY. Glasses up, everyone. (*Stands next to* POLLY. EVY *seems to be unaware of the tension in the room that she is causing. Once on alcohol, she enters a world of her own.*)

JIMMY. (*Holds up glass.*) To Toby. . . . Whom we all love and cherish. Happy Birthday.

POLLY. Happy Birthday, Toby. (*They all drink.*)

TOBY. Thank you.

EVY. . . . That's the toast? Sounds like she died of leukemia. "Fifty dollars donation in memory of Toby Landau, who we loved and cherished." . . . She's alive, for Christ's sakes, tell her what a great broad she is.

TOBY. It was a lovely toast, Evy . . . and I'm very touched.

EVY. . . . You're a great broad, Toby, I want you to know it. Only one who came to see me in the hospital. I'll never forget you for that. . . .

TOBY. Evy, stop, I'm going to cry again.

Evy. I don't care if you whistle "Dixie" through your ass, I'm telling you I love you. . . . (Toby *looks at* Polly.) Woops, sorry, Polly. Mother's being naughty. (*Pours some more wine in her glass.*)

Jimmy. Evy, will you give me that bottle?

Evy. When it's empty, pussycat.

Polly. Mother, should I get the cake now?

Evy. I'll *tell* you when to get the cake. I'm not ready for the cake yet. What the hell's the big rush with the cake? I didn't rent it, I bought it outright. . . . I'm still telling Toby how much I love her. (*Points to* Toby *with the hand holding the glass. The wine spills over and on* Toby's *dress.*) Oh, Christ, Jesus, I'm sorry. . . . (*Tries wiping it with her hand.*) On your birthday, got you right in the crotch. . . . Polly, get me a Kleenex or something.

Toby. It's alright, it'll dry.

Evy. It's ruined. Your two hundred and fifty dollar dress is ruined. . . . Listen, I want you to take my mink coat. I paid thirty-two hundred bucks for it in 1941, you can get about four dollars for it now and I'll pay you a little bit each week. (*She's still rubbing* Toby's *dress.*)

Toby. Evy, it's alright, it's an old dress.

Evy. No kidding? I'll buy it from you. What do you want, about twenty dollars? I mean it's not worth more, it's got a Goddamned wine stain right in the front.

Jimmy. Polly, why don't you get the cake?

Evy. (*Screams.*) Don't you touch that cake! I'm M.C.-ing this party. . . .

Toby. Evy, please don't drink any more.

Jimmy. Evy, I'm asking you nicely for the last time. Put down the wine.

Evy. I am. I'm putting it down as fast as I can. (*Crosses to* Toby.) . . . Listen, I got a first-class idea. Why don't you two move in with us? We don't need anybody else. . . . Just us four girls. What do you say?

Toby. (*About to fall apart.*) Evy, I've got to go (*Crossing.*) Thank you for the party.

Evy. What party? Two salted peanuts, everyone took turns crying and you fink out on me.

Toby. Evy, I can't sit here and watch what's happening. (*At the door.*) Polly, take care of her. I'll call you in the morning. . . . (*To* Evy.) Evy—I'm sorry if I did this to you. (*She can't say any more, but turns and runs out.*)

Evy. (*Calls out.*) Wait a minute. Your present. I didn't give you your present. (*Looks up.*) Polly, get her back.

Polly. She's gone, Mother.

Evy. (*Playfully goes to* Jimmy.) I believe this is your dance, Colonel Sanders, and by the way, I love your finger-lickin' chicken.

Jimmy. Evy, Evy, you stupid bitch.

Evy. Hey, hey, watch that kind of talk. I have a daughter here someplace.

Jimmy. Then why do you act this way in front of her?

Polly. Jimmy, it's alright.

Jimmy. It's *not* alright. She's drunk and disgusting and she doesn't give a damn about herself or anyone else. Well, then damn it, neither do I. Go on. Finish the bottle. Finish the whole Goddamn case, for all I care.

Evy. Okay, buster, you just talked yourself out of an opening night party.

Jimmy. And you just drank yourself out of a couple of friends. I don't want to see you anymore, Evy. I swear to God. I am through. Finished forever, I've *had* it. . . . Goodbye, Polly, I'm sorry. (*Goes quickly to door.*)

Evy. How about a little kiss goodbye? (*Grabs his arm.*) Come on, one little kiss on the lips. It'll make all the New York papers.

Jimmy. Let go of me, damn it! (*Wrenches from* Evy *and runs out, leaving the door open.* Evy *rushes to the door and yells out.*)

Evy. (*Pleading.*) Jimmy! . . . Jimmy, come back, I'm sorry. . . . Jimmy, don't leave me, you're the only man in my life. (*But he's gone. . . . Comes back into the*

apartment. Tries to compose herself in front of POLLY.)
. . . I guess this would be a good time to get the cake.

POLLY. I'm not hungry. I've got homework to do. I'll clean up later.

EVY. Oh, you're mad at me. I don't know what I did, but you're mad at me, right?

POLLY. I'm not mad at you, Mother.

EVY. What then? You're ashamed? Ashamed of your sweet little old mother because she had two tiny glasses of domestic wine?

POLLY. I'm not ashamed.

EVY. *Then what are you?*

POLLY. I'm sorry . . . I'm just plain sorry. (*Looks at* EVY, *then slowly goes into bedroom and closes the door behind her.* EVY *stands there.*)

EVY. (*Loudly.*) Sorry for what? For me? Well, don't be sorry for me because I don't need your Goddamned teenage pity. . . . I'm terrific, baby, haven't you noticed? Cost me 27 hundred bucks and I'm skinny and terrific and I can have any dirty old man in the neighborhood. . . . (*Suddenly softening.*) Oh, Jesus, Polly, I'm sorry. . . . (*Crosses to bedroom door.*) Polly, don't be mad. . . . Come on out, we'll have our own private party. . . . Look! Look, I'm gonna put on some music. (*Crosses to record player.*) I've just had a request to play one of my old numbers. (*Takes out her album.*) Come listen to Mother sing when she was a big star, darling. (*Puts record on machine.*) Well, not exactly a big star. . . . But I once had a sandwich named after me at the Stage Delicatessen. . . . (*The MUSIC STARTS. . . . We hear* EVY *singing. . . . She stands there listening, drink-from wine glass.*) . . . That's not bad, is it? . . . It's not bad. . . . It's not *thrilling* but it's not bad. . . . (*Sings along, looks around room.*) This is about the same size audiences I used to get. . . . (*Crosses to bedroom door.*) Polly, please come out. . . . I don't want to listen to me all by myself. . . . Polly? (*No answer. Looks at*

the phone.) I am *not* going to listen all by myself. . . .
(*Crosses to phone. . . . Takes a deep breath and dials.
Into phone:*) . . . Hello? Lou? . . . You alone? . . .
Guess who wants to come over to your place?

THE CURTAIN FALLS

ACT THREE

The following morning about 11 A.M. It's Saturday.

AT RISE: POLLY *is seated on the piano bench staring aimlessly and worriedly.* TOBY, *in a polo coat over pajamas, sits on chair, nervously smoking.*

TOBY. I'm not worried.

POLLY. You've told me that since eight o'clock this morning, Toby.

TOBY. (*Puffs again.*) She's alright. She's done this before. I am not worried.

POLLY. Is that why you've had nine cigarettes since you got here?

TOBY. I have other problems on my mind besides your mother's disappearance. (*Puffs.*) If I get nicotine stains on my teeth, I'll never forgive her.

POLLY. She just walks out and disappears all night without saying a word. Where the hell could she be?

TOBY. Don't swear, darling, your mother wouldn't like it. . . . You really should get some sleep, angel. You're going to get little ugly puffy rings under your eyes.

POLLY. I'm sorry, Toby. I've never gone through this before.

TOBY. She's put me through it for twelve years. That's why I wear such heavy makeup. Underneath this is my mother.

POLLY. (*Determined.*) I'm not going to forgive her, Toby, I swear. . . . The minute I hear she's alright, I'm not going to forgive her. (*Starts to cry, rushes into bedroom and closes the door behind her.* TOBY *picks up her coffee cup and starts to cross into kitchen when the door opens. It's* EVY, *hiding her face.*)

TOBY. Well, good morning.

64

Evy. That's entirely possible.

Toby. Do you know what time it is?

Evy. November?

Toby. Evy!

Evy. Later, Toby, I have to go to the john.

Toby. I refuse to talk to your unbrushed hair all morning. Turn around and look at me. (Evy *turns around revealing a black-and-blue eye*.) Oh, God . . . your eye. Evy, what have you done?

Evy. You want to be my friend, Toby, no questions and no sympathy. I'm alright.

Toby. I don't think I *want* to hear about it.

Evy. Where's Polly?

Toby. She's been up all night calling everyone. I made her go in and lie down.

Evy. Well, if she sleeps for three weeks I may get away with it.

Toby. You don't seem to be acting much like a woman who just got beaten up.

Evy. I didn't get beaten, Toby, just punched. One clean, little punch, I never felt it.

Toby. Really? Have you seen what you look like?

Evy. Compared to you, what difference does it make? . . . I'm alright, I promise you.

Toby. Sit down, let me put some ice on it.

Evy. I've already had medical attention. A dog licked my face while I was down.

Toby. Who did it?

Evy. What difference does it make?

Toby. Because I feel responsible.

Evy. Come on, Toby. I got what I asked for last night because I wasn't getting anything else. (*Sits.*) Alright, I'm sitting. Are you happy now?

Toby. How can I be happy when your face is half smashed in? How many places did you have to go before you found what you were looking for?

Evy. Just one. If there's one thing I know how to do, it's shop.

TOBY. (*Turns away.*) Oh, Christ, Evy, sometimes you disgust me.

EVY. That seems to be the general feeling around town.

TOBY. It was Lou Tanner, wasn't it?

EVY. That's him. The man I love.

TOBY. Jesus, I knew it. There was always something about him that frightened me. You could see it in his eyes.

EVY. Never mind the eyes, it's the big fist you gotta watch. . . . I wouldn't hate you if you left me alone now, Toby.

TOBY. Why did you go there, Evy?

EVY. He plays requests, I was lonesome.

TOBY. Why did you start drinking yesterday? Everything was going so good for you. Why, Evy?

EVY. What did you want, a nice, simple answer? When I was six years old my father didn't take me to the circus. . . . How the hell do I know why I do anything?

TOBY. Didn't you learn anything in ten weeks at the hospital?

EVY. The doctor tried to explain but I was too busy making a pass at him. . . . If I knew, Toby, would it make any difference?

TOBY. It would help.

EVY. If you haven't eaten in three months you don't want a description of food, you want a little hot something in the plate.

TOBY. And did you get your fill last night, Evy? Did you get your little hot something in the plate?

EVY. No, but we negotiated for a while. . . .

TOBY. With someone like that? A deadbeat musician who doesn't give a damn about hitting some drunken woman.

EVY. You just don't get hit like that, you gotta ask for it. . . . I happened to make a bad choice. I broke his guitar. I smashed it against the refrigerator, handed him the pieces and said, "Now you can look for work you're equipped to do." I thought it was cute, the man has no sense of humor.

TOBY. The truth. Evy. When he was beating you, did you enjoy it?

EVY. Well, for a second there I said to myself, it hurts like hell—but it sure beats indifference. (*Gets up.*) Is there anything in the kitchen? I'm always hungry after a fight.

TOBY. (*Angrily.*) What fight? There was no fight. You just stood there and let him beat the crap out of you.

EVY. That's right, pussycat.

TOBY. The way you let *everybody* beat the crap out of you.

EVY. Same as you. Only Marty doesn't punch, he just walks out on you. In your own adorable way, you're no better off than I am.

TOBY. (*Still angry.*) At least my face isn't beaten to a pulp.

EVY. Terrific. You spent forty years being gorgeous and all you've got to show for it is a turned up little nose. . . . We cried for you yesterday, today is my turn.

TOBY. At least I've *tried* to make things work. I've at least made the *effort.*

EVY. The only effort you make is opening your compact. If you powdered Marty once in a while instead of your face, you'd be wearing *his* pajamas now instead of yours.

TOBY. I powdered my Goddamned face because I was afraid every time Marty looked at me too closely. Afraid he'd see what I was becoming.

EVY. Terrific. Why don't you spend the rest of your life in the Beverly Hills Polo Lounge? You can put on a Shirley Temple dress and suck a lollipop. . . . And next year you'll have an affair with the book publisher's grandson. . . .

TOBY. Go to hell.

EVY. Toby, you know I love you. We're the same kind

of broads. We both manage to screw up everything. . . .
The only difference is, you dressed better doing it.

TOBY. Damn you, Evy. Damn you for being so Goddamned honest all the time. Who needs the truth if this
is what it gets you?

EVY. Listen, I'm willing to live a lie. As far as I'm
concerned, I'm twenty-two with a cute little behind. Now
find me a fellow who believes it.

TOBY. You're not twenty-two, you're forty-three. And
you're an alcoholic with no sense of morality or responsi-
bility. You've never had a lasting relationship with anyone who wasn't as weak or as helpless as yourself. So you
have friends like Jimmy and me. Misfits who can't do any
more than pick up your discarded clothes and empty
glasses. We all hold each other up because none of us has
the strength to do it alone. And lovers like Lou Tanner
whose only talent is to beat your bloody face in and
leave you when something better comes along. I know
what I am, Evy. I don't like it and I never have. So I
cover the outside with Helena Rubenstein. I use little
makeup jars, you use quart bottles. . . . And poor Jimmy
uses a little of both. . . . Some terrific people. . . . But
by some strange miracle, in there— (*Indicating bedroom.*) —is a girl who is crazy in love with you because
she's too young to know any better. . . . But keep it up,
Evy, and she'll get to know better before you can say
Jack Daniels. . . . The way I see it, you've got two
choices: Either get a book on how to be a mature, responsible person . . . or get her out of here before you
destroy her chance to become one. . . . There's your
honesty and truth, Evy. . . . It's a perfect fit. How do
you like it?

EVY. Actually, I was looking for something in a blue.

TOBY. That's the first time in my entire life I ever told
anyone off. I think I'm going to be sick.

EVY. Look who's getting to be a real person. (*Crosses,
puts her arms around* TOBY.) Next week, with a little
luck, you'll throw away the eyelashes.

TOBY. Don't hate me, Evy. I still need a little help from my friends. Tell me you don't hate me.

EVY. *Hate* you? I'm having trouble seeing you.

TOBY. So am I. But the picture's getting clearer. . . . Come on, let me put something on your disgusting eye.

EVY. I got a big scene to play with Polly, I don't need an audience. Go on home.

TOBY. I can't. Marty's still there collecting some papers and things.

EVY. You want to take some advice from a drunk? Go home, wash the crap off your face, put on a sloppy house-dress and bring him a TV dinner. What the hell could you lose?

TOBY. Nothing. . . . Wouldn't it be funny if you were right?

EVY. Of course I'm right. I'm always right. That's how I got where I am today.

TOBY. Jesus, I suddenly hate my face. . . . What I'd love to do is get rid of the Goddamned thing.

EVY. No, you don't. You're going to send it to me by messenger. *This* lady is still in trouble.

TOBY. I'm going. (*Crosses to door.*) I'm scared to death, but I'm going. . . . I suddenly feel ten years older. . . . Look, Evy. Look at the pretty old lady.

EVY. You'll love it. Little boys'll help you across the street.

TOBY. (*Opens door.*) Evy, don't tell Polly the truth about what happened. Lie a little. Protect her. That's what mothers are for.

EVY. I'll say I was walking along West End Avenue and was hit by the Eastern Airlines shuttle to Boston.

TOBY. It needs work. I'll call you from home later. I have to stop off first and blow up my beauty parlor. (*Exits, closing door behind her.*)

(EVY *sits there a moment.* POLLY *comes out.*)

POLLY. Good morning.

Evy. (*Her back to her.*) You're up. Did you get any sleep?

Polly. No. There was terrible news on the radio. Someone was hit by an Eastern Airlines shuttle to Boston.

Evy. (*Turns around and reveals herself to* Polly.) It was me. . . . How do you like it?

Polly. Wow. It's terrific. Goes very nice with this neighborhood. Listen, I don't have any steak to put on that. Will bacon and eggs do?

Evy. You're not going to yell at me, is that it?

Polly. I thought you were going to yell at me. I didn't go to sleep last night either. (*Suddenly* Polly *rushes into* Evy's *arms.*) Oh, Evy, Evy, I'm so glad to see you.

Evy. (*Winces.*) The jaw, the jaw, watch the jaw.

Polly. Listen, don't tell Toby. I promised her I wouldn't forgive you.

Evy. She's not even my friend anymore. She's too old for me.

Polly. Starting tomorrow I'm not speaking to you. But I'm so glad to see you today.

Evy. (*Pulls her to sofa.*) You got to admit, it's not a dull place to live.

Polly. Listen, we're not going to discuss it. It never even happened. Can I get you anything?

Evy. If you move from me, you'll get worse than I got. (*Hugs her. . . . There's a moment's pause.*)

Polly. I had a drink.

Evy. What?

Polly. I made myself a scotch at two o'clock in the morning. The Excedrin P.M. wasn't working and I had to do something to stop the throbbing in my head.

Evy. Did it stop?

Polly. No, but it made it bearable. . . . Is that what it's like, Evy? Is that what it does? Make things bearable?

Evy. (*Nods.*) Mm hmm. And if you take enough, it even stops the throbbing. . . . Jesus, three weeks and I turned my daughter into a lush.

POLLY. I hated it. I'll never take another drop in my life. From now on I'm sticking with marijuana.

EVY. That's Momma's good girl.

POLLY. (*Pulls back.*) Hey, listen, we better get moving. We have a lunch date in a half an hour, remember?

EVY. What lunch date?

POLLY. I told you last night. With Daddy, at Rumplemayer's.

EVY. Are you serious? With me looking like Rocky Graziano? He'll send you to a convent.

POLLY. We could put something on it. Some powder or something. Or you could wear a hat. With a little veil.

EVY. I could sit behind a big screen and talk through a microphone. I can't go to Rumplemayer's looking like this.

POLLY. We'll think of something. . . . How about you just did a Tareyton commercial?

EVY. How about just forgetting it?

POLLY. We can't. He's expecting you. What about a pair of dark sunglasses?

EVY. It's not just the eye, baby. I have a hangover and the shakes. When I start spilling water on his lap, he's gonna notice something.

POLLY. But if you don't show up, he'll think something is wrong.

EVY. How right could things be if you show up with a punchy mother? . . . Is Melissa coming too?

POLLY. Felicia.

EVY. Felicia. . . . Can you picture that scene? I walk into Rumplemayer's looking like a dead fish and she clicks in her coffee and he spits in his sherbet.

POLLY. She's not coming. It's just the three of us. He wants to talk to us together. I promised him that when I came here.

EVY. Well, unpromise him, I'm not going.

POLLY. (*Giving up.*) Okay . . . I'll tell him you're not feeling well. I'll figure out something. We'll do it again next week. (POLLY *goes for her coat.*) In the meantime, will you see a doctor?

EVY. Yes, angel.

POLLY. When?

EVY. As soon as I look better.

POLLY. I'll bring you back a coffee malted and a toy. . . . Get some sleep, I'll be home in an hour. (*Opens door, about to go.*)

EVY. Polly!

POLLY. (*Stops, turns.*) Yes?

EVY. . . . Maybe you'd better not make another date for next week. . . . Not yet, anyway.

POLLY. You'll be alright by next Saturday. It's not that bad, really.

EVY. It's not the eye I'm worried about. . . . It's the rest of the person.

POLLY. (*Closes door.*) What are you saying, Mother?

EVY. Nothing, baby. . . . It's just that I don't know if I'm pulled together yet. . . . You saw how suddenly everything unraveled yesterday. . . . They warned me in the hospital that after a while I might expect some sort of setback.

POLLY. Okay, you had a little setback. . . . Onwards and upwards.

EVY. Didn't you ever hear of downwards?

POLLY. I've heard of it. You wouldn't like it there. It's worse than Garden City.

EVY. Polly, I don't think I'm ready for you yet. I don't think I can handle it.

POLLY. Handle what? I put on three pounds since I'm here.

EVY. Mostly Sara Lee's cheesecake. . . .

POLLY. I'm alive, I'm healthy, I'm not floating on my back. What's wrong, Mother?

EVY. Mother, heh? Some mother. . . . When am I here? I'm out all day doing absolutely nothing and I still manage to come home late. I saw you more when you didn't live with me.

POLLY. I'm not complaining.

EVY. Well, complain, damn it! What are you so forgiving for? I was a slob last night. A pig and a slob.

POLLY. It only happened once.

EVY. Wait, it's early, the new schedule didn't come out yet. . . . Besides, it didn't happen once. . . . Before last night there was an occasional beer on a wet, lonely afternoon, a couple of glasses of wine on a sunny, lonely afternoon . . . and once, after a really rotten Swedish movie, a double vodka.

POLLY. Okay, so forget downwards and upwards. We'll try sideways for a while.

EVY. What we'll try is that you'll go home for a couple of weeks until I pull myself together. That's all, baby, just a couple of weeks. And when you get back, I'll be a regular Doris Day type mother, okay? Freckles and everything.

POLLY. If I leave now you know where you'll be in two weeks. You still have another eye left.

EVY. Polly, please—

POLLY. And in two weeks you'll find a reason to add another two weeks. And before you know it, Evy, I'll be all grown up and won't even need you anymore.

EVY. Listen, you weren't in such bad shape when you got here.

POLLY. (*Angrily.*) Is it such a Goddamned big deal to need somebody? If you can need a bottle of scotch or a Lou Tanner, why can't you need me?

EVY. I do need you, baby. I just don't want to use you. Like the rest of the company around here. . . . In a few weeks you'll know the regular routine. . . . You'll get a two hour storm warning then wait in your bedroom until all the bottles are empty and all the glasses are smashed and in the mornings there'll be a lot of Alka Seltzers and black coffee and crying and forgiving and promises and we'll live happily ever after for two more weeks. And in a year or so you won't even mind it. . . . Like Jimmy and Toby. . . . But they have nothing better to do with their lives. You're only seventeen.

POLLY. They're just friends, I'm your daughter.

EVY. You get my point?

POLLY. No! . . . What *is* it, Evy? Am I getting kicked out because you're afraid I'm going to grow up to be a crutch instead of a person? Or do you just want to be left alone so there's no one here to lock up the liquor cabinet?

EVY. You're going to be late for Rumplemayer's.

POLLY. *Screw* Rumplemayer's!

EVY. (*Looks at* POLLY *and smiles.*) . . . My, my. . . . Look how quickly you can learn if you pay attention.

POLLY. I'm sorry.

EVY. Go on. Please, Polly. Go now.

POLLY. Don't I get to argue my side?

EVY. Not today. Mother is hungover.

POLLY. I see. . . . Okay. . . . If the room's not for rent, it's not for rent. . . . When do you want me out?

EVY. Alright, let's not get maudlin. . . . You're not moving to the Philippines, just 86th and Madison.

POLLY. (*Nods.*) I'll be back for my stuff later.

EVY. I'll get everything ready. If nothing else, I'm a terrific packer.

POLLY. I'm glad you finally found something to keep you busy. (*Glares at* EVY, *then crosses to the door. She turns and looks at* EVY.)

EVY. . . . What?

POLLY. I was just wondering if you were going to say goodbye.

EVY. Not unless you want to see a major breakdown.

POLLY. Never mind. It's the thought that counts.

(*PHONE RINGS.* POLLY *exits, closing the door behind her.* EVY *is at her low ebb. She crosses to her mink coat and takes out pint bottle of liquor. She pours it into glass and crosses and sits on chair, her legs up on stool. PHONE STOPS. She drinks. . . . The*

DOORBELL RINGS. She pays no attention. We hear JIMMY's *voice.*)

JIMMY. Evy? . . . Evy, it's Jimmy. . . . Evy, I know you're there, I just saw Polly on the stairs. (*She drinks.*) Damn it, Evy, answer me.

EVY. Evy's not here. She moved. This is a recording.

JIMMY. (*Pounds on door.*) Evy, I'll break this door down, I swear. . . . I know what you're doing in there. (*Pause.*) Three seconds, Evy. If it's not open in three seconds, I'm breaking it down. (*She drinks. Suddenly the door breaks down and* JIMMY's *body hurtles into the room and onto the floor.* EVY *looks at him.*)

EVY. Jesus, I didn't think you could do it.

JIMMY. (*Gets up, moves to her.*) I knew it. I knew you'd be here with a glass in your hand drinking your-self— (*Notices her eye.*) Oh, my God. Look at you. Look at your face.

EVY. If you're going to throw up, use the bathroom.

JIMMY. He beat you. The son of a bitch beat you.

EVY. And if you try to take this away from me, I'll show you how it was done.

JIMMY. It was Lou Tanner, wasn't it? Toby just called me. I'll find him. If it takes me the rest of my life, I'll track that son of a bitch down and kill him.

EVY. Once he hears, he'll never sleep another night. . . . Will you close the drapes, Jimmy? And then leave me alone like a good boy.

JIMMY. (*Closes the drapes.*) Sure. I'll leave you alone. I turn my back for two seconds, they have to call the emergency squad. . . . What happened? How did he beat you?

EVY. How many ways are there? You get hit and you fall down.

JIMMY. Look at your eye. What did he hit you with, his guitar?

EVY. No, the guitar was the preliminaries.

JIMMY. I want to know the details, Evy. How did he beat you?

EVY. Since when are you interested in sports?

JIMMY. (*In a fit of anger, he pushes her.*) You think it's so Goddamned funny, go look at yourself.

EVY. How come everybody's so physical lately? Where were you all when I needed you?

JIMMY. Have you called the police? Have you seen a doctor? What have you done?

EVY. Outside of bleeding, not very much. You want the Goddamned case, I give it to you. If you're interested in my welfare, get me another glass, then turn out the light and get out of here. Leave me alone, Jimmy, please. . . .

JIMMY. . . . I'll never forgive myself for running out last night. . . . Never. (*Turns off alcove light. Crosses back to* EVY *on sofa, puts arm on her.*) . . . It's alright, baby. . . . We got through it before, we'll get through it again.

EVY. . . . And again . . . and again . . .

JIMMY. Feel better?

EVY. Much. . . . There was this movie with Jean Simmons.

JIMMY. English or American?

EVY. English. And she was in love with this boy.

JIMMY. Stewart Granger? David Niven? Michael Wilding?

EVY. He was very short with blond hair.

JIMMY. Short English actor. Blond hair. Alec Guiness? Michael Caine?

EVY. Miles? Mills?

JIMMY. Mills. John Mills. "Great Expectations" directed by David Lean with Valerie Hobson, John Mills, Francis Sullivan and introducing Jean Simmons. What about it?

EVY. She had this crazy old aunt who spent forty years in a wedding dress. The boy she loved never showed up for the wedding. Never saw him again but she never changed a thing for forty years. Cobwebs on the Goddamned wedding cake. . . . And she never went out into the city and she closed all the shutters and never let the sun into the house. . . . She was covered with dust, this crazy old broad. . . . Sat there in the dark, rotting and falling apart. . . . Mice nibbling away at the wedding gifts . . . and as I watched her I remembered saying to myself, "She doesn't seem so crazy to me."

JIMMY. Martita Hunt played the aunt. Her dress caught fire and she burned to death, screaming on the floor. Try not to think of it.

EVY. I'm okay. There ain't no cobwebs on me.

JIMMY. What can I get you? Let me get you something. Coffee? A sandwich? Something to drink? I'll even let you have a real drink, how about that?

EVY. It's no fun that way. I have to sneak it.

JIMMY. If I go away, if I leave you alone, will you take a nap?

EVY. For you? Anything.

JIMMY. Not for me. For yourself.

EVY. Well, we'll split it. I'll sleep a little for you and a little for me. . . . Will you turn the rest of the lights out? (JIMMY *crosses and turns out another light.*) I can still see you, Charley. (*He turns out the remaining light. The room is almost in total darkness except for the light in the kitchen.*) That's better.

JIMMY. (*Moves in the dark, hits stool.*) Christ, now I can't find the door.

EVY. Don't worry about it, darling. Come to bed.

JIMMY. Bitch, go to sleep. (*Has found the door and opens it.*) . . . I'll take a walk in Central Park. If I'm not back in an hour, I found true happiness. (*Goes, closing door behind him.*)

EVY. And get something for me, you bastard. (*She is alone. She gets up, crosses to record player and switches on record again. Her voice is heard singing the song from last night. She pours herself another drink and crosses back to piano, drinking and listening. Suddenly, the front door opens and* POLLY *stands there in doorway, looking into dark room, worriedly.*)

POLLY. (*Concerned.*) Mother? Are you alright?

EVY. (*In shadows.*) What are you doing here? (*Gets up quickly.*)

POLLY. I forgot my wallet. I don't have carfare. . . . What's the matter with the lights?

EVY. Nothing. I have a headache.

POLLY. Well, no wonder. It's so depressing in here. Like some ghost movie on the late show.

EVY. (*Turns off record.*) "Great Expectations" directed by David Lean. (POLLY *switches on a light.* EVY *winces from the glare.*) Christ, do you have to do that?

POLLY. I have to find my wallet. I'll be out in a minute. (*Starts to look around and then finds the half-empty liquor botle on the table where* EVY *was sitting. She holds up bottle, turns and looks at* EVY.)

EVY. Well, if that's your wallet, take it and go.

POLLY. It's not my wallet. It looks like yours.

EVY. Alright, what do you want, a reward? Put it down and go. Can't you see I'm trying to take a nap?

POLLY. Some nap. (*Turns on another light and then another lamp.*)

EVY. What are you doing? I don't want those lights on. Leave those lights alone.

POLLY. So you can sit here in the dark, drinking?

EVY. It's not hard, I know where my lips are. (POLLY *crosses to windows.*) Get away from those curtains.

POLLY. (*Opening first curtain.*) Sitting here in the dark like some crazy spook. I have a crazy spook for a mother.

EVY. And I have a disrespectful pain in the ass for a daughter. That's what I get for sending you to a private school.

POLLY. (*Opening other curtains.*) Why don't you get some bats and owls in here? Fly around the room on a broomstick. Crazy old spook mother.

EVY. Where's my pocketbook? Take a taxi. Buy a car, only get out of here.

POLLY. And you can sit here and finish the rest of the bottle, right?

EVY. I wasn't drinking, I was meditating.

POLLY. Ten more minutes and you'd have meditated right out on the floor. . . . That's why you want to be alone.

EVY. I'm not alone. Jimmy was here. And he's coming back in an hour.

POLLY. And he'll do whatever you ask him, right? Turn out the lights, seal up the windows, refill your bottles? Anything as long as Evy's happy.

EVY. Yes! Yes, dammit! Now get out of here and leave me alone!

POLLY. That's why you kicked me out. Because you're afraid of me. Aren't you, Mother? Admit you're afraid of me.

EVY. Don't test me. One more word, you'll walk into Rumplemayer's looking like me.

POLLY. Go ahead, hit me. I don't mind a little pain, Mother. It sure beats indifference!

EVY. Jesus, you can't say a word around here without you listening at the door.

POLLY. I don't have to listen through the door. When you're drunk, they can hear you in Brazil.

EVY. I won't stand for this kind of talk.

POLLY. Yes, you will. You'll stand for anything!

EVY. Stop it! Stop it, Polly!

POLLY. Then *make* me! Do something about it!

EVY. I won't be talked to this way. I swear, you're going to get it, Polly.

POLLY. I'm waiting. Please! Give it to me. Evy!

EVY. Not from me. From your father. I swear to God, I'm going to tell your father.

POLLY. (*Yells.*) *Then tell him!* Tell him what I've become after three weeks. You want things to tell him about, Evy? (*Picks up liquor glass.*) Here! (*Hurls it against the bookcase, smashing it to pieces.*) Alright? Now come to Rumplemayer's and tell him. . . . Only please don't sit in the dark for the rest of your life. (*Has burst into tears. She kneels, crying. . . . *EVY *finds it difficult to go to her. . . . Then it's quiet.*)

EVY. . . . Couldn't he have picked a nice out-of-the-way restaurant in Nebraska?

POLLY. (*Turns around hopefully.*) You mean you've changed your mind?

EVY. I didn't change anything.

POLLY. Alright, don't change your mind. Just change your dress. You can change your mind on the way over.

EVY. (*Looks to heaven.*) She's *his* daughter. I have too much class for a daughter like this.

POLLY. Listen, how about if I don't come back as a daughter? I could be a house guest. I'll just stay till I'm thirty-five, then get out, I promise.

EVY. Didn't we just settle all that?

POLLY. You and your daughter settled all that. I'm a stranger. Why don't you show me the rest of the apartment?

EVY. (*Again up to heaven.*) Who is she? Who sent this monster to torment me?

POLLY. Felicia. She can't stand any of us. (POLLY *has clearly won.* EVY *wilts, opens her arms and* POLLY *runs in.*)

EVY. Oh, God, I'm not strong enough to resist you. . . . I suppose I'll be speaking at your school next week.

POLLY. We've got fifteen minutes. What can we do with your face in fifteen minutes?

EVY. Christ, I don't know. There's a one-hour cleaner around the corner.

POLLY. You've known Toby Landau for twelve years and you never heard of makeup? Come on, sit down.

EVY. We'll never get away with it.

POLLY. Yes, you will. (*Takes out compact from her purse.*)

EVY. I'll get twenty years for impersonating a mother.

POLLY. Good. We'll share a cell together.

Evy. The hell we will. I'm forty-three years old. Someday I'm getting my own place.

Polly. (*Starts to apply makeup under eye.*) Now remember. Once we get there, don't be nervous. Just be cool and nonchalant.

Evy. What if I do something stupid like eat the ice cream with a fork?

Polly. Then I'll eat mine with a fork. He'll look at us, think *he's* wrong, and eat *his* with a fork. . . . Try not to move.

Evy. Who would believe this? A middle-aged drunk with a black eye is worried about impressing a forty-seven-year-old spitter.

Polly. Alright, I'm through.

Evy. How does it look?

Polly. Much better.

Evy. (*Picks up mirror and looks at herself.*) It's *not* better. It looks like I was punched in the eye and someone put makeup on it.

Polly. If we don't get away with it, we'll tell him the truth. He's a terrific person, Evy. He'll understand the truth.

Evy. About Lou Tanner?

Polly. No. The Eastern Airlines shuttle to Boston. Come on. Let's get a decent dress on you. You look like you're collecting for UNICEF.

Evy. Polly.

Polly. What?

Evy. When I grow up, I want to be just like you.

CURTAIN

PROPERTY PLOT

ACT ONE

D. R.:

Small portable TV on chair by D. window
Telephone table (pedestal base, low, round)

On it:
6 to 8 phone messages
Ashtray
Writing pad and pencil
Telephone and address book
Telephone book on floor

Chair (small) facing U

On it:
Black telephone

R.:

Windows, with curtains, drapes and shades
Plants (wilted, dying and dead)

Piano (keyboard open and facing D and R.)

On it:
Framed photographs (assorted sizes)
Piano bench with music on it and in it
High stool (inside piano curve)

R. C.:

Coffee table (low, round)

On it:
Brass container
Two books of matches

Under it:
Sheet music

Sofa sectional (R. of coffee table)

Behind it:
Sheet music on floor
Sofa throw pillow (on floor front of sofa)
Armchair (U of coffee table)
Stool (L. of coffee table)

82

u. c. (ALCOVE) :

Armchair (against R. wall with box on it)

Behind it:
Newspapers on floor

Desk (against L. wall)

On it:
Bundle of unopened mail
Dressing

Under it:
Wicker basket

Desk chair

u. wall :
Photographs and memorabilia
Shelf :
With records, turntable
Microphone, dressing

Below desk:
Wooden chair with phono speaker and two cardboard boxes
on it

U. L. :

Monk's chair (R. of front door with umbrella leaning against
it)
Standing hat rack (L. of front door)
Umbrella stand (back of hat rack)

L :

Kitchen table (round)

On it:
Bookmatches

High-back dining chair (L. of table)

On it:
Sheepskin coat (JIMMY)

In it:
Envelope with unemployment book and money (U.
pocket)

Kitchen chair (R. of table)

Counter shelf

On it:
Amber cigarette container (empty)
Assorted glasses
Ashtray
Dish towel
Box of paper napkins
High stool (in front of counter)
Wastebasket (on floor next to stool)

D. L.:

Cupboard (built-in)

On it:
Dishes, dressing

Kitchen chair (D. of cupboard)

On it:
Shoulder/tote bag (JIMMY)

In bag:
Saccharin bottle
Play script
Newspaper

U. L.:

Kitchen:
Refrigerator
Shelf or counter

On it:
Can opener
Vase of flowers in sink
2 ashtrays in sink
Coffeepot with coffee
Serving tray with 2 mugs, 1 cup and saucer, 3 spoor
Box of Kleenex
Dressing

Inside kitchen window:
Shelf or table with 2 bottles champagne, 1 empty glass

U. R.:

Bedroom:
Bed and dressing

Bookshelf with books
Lamp
Small table (D. wall)

PROPERTY TABLE—Off stage L.:

2 hardback novels (contemporary)
2 bags of groceries
1 bag with 1 six-pack of Coke, 1 six-pack of Canada Dry Gingerale
1 apple
1 Saks Fifth Avenue shopping bag

In it:

2 bottles champagne (unopened)
2 packages Philip Morris cigarettes
1 Gucci box
2 jars of dry roasted peanuts
1 cake box (tied)

1 package cigarettes (opened) with 4 cigarettes (JIMMY)
1 bookmatches (JIMMY)
1 package cigarettes (opened) with 1 cigarette (TOBY's purse)
1 overnight suitcase (EVY)
1 large suitcase (POLLY) with prop clothing
1 pint of scotch with food-colored water 1/2 full
1 front door key (POLLY)

END OF ACT ONE

INTERMISSION

STRIKE:

Messages from phone table
Dead plants
Vase of flowers
Empty packs cigarettes
Tray with coffeepot, mugs
Coffee can and opener (kitchen)
2 suitcases and clothing (bedroom)
2 novels from bookcase
All newspapers and boxes
Clean and replace all ashtrays

SET:

TV set to alcove shelf
New plants to windows and piano
6 rock records on coffee table, 2 out of jackets
Furniture to Act Two marks
Box of Kleenex on desk (U. end)
Tablecloth and ashtray on kitchen table
Composition book on armchair

END OF ACT TWO

INTERMISSION

STRIKE:

Gucci box
2 jars of peanuts
Cigarette packages
Dirty glasses
Champagne bottles
Cake box
All cigarettes from container but 1
Saks shopping bag
Book (bedroom)
Green pillow from sofa

SET:

1 cigarette on coffee table (Toby)
1 coffee mug (coffee table)
Ashtray with 8 or 9 butts (coffee table)
Toby's Act Three purse on coffee table
Furniture to ACT THREE MARKS

PERSONAL PROPS:

Jimmy—Wristwatch, wallet, ten dollar bill, twenty-eight cents
change
Polly—purse
Evy—purse
Toby—3 purses

FURNITURE LIST

R.:
Plant pedestal

D. R.:
Telephone table, pedestal base, round
1 small chair
1 dining chair
Apartment grand piano (5'2")
Piano bench
Bar stool

R. C.:
Sofa sectional, curved, no arms
Low coffee table—42 inches
Small armchair, wooden arms, pillow on seat
Low wicker stool

U. C.:
Small writing table (desk)
Small chair
Upholstered armchair
Wall mirror
Stereo speakers

U. L. C.:
Standing coat rack

U. L.:
1 bar stool

D. L.:
Dining table (kitchen table), 36" round, pedestal base
1 monk's chair
1 cane-seat, ladder-back chair
2 unmatched dining chairs

Bedroom:
Bed
Small table

Kitchen:
Refrigerator
Small table

Lighting fixtures:
- 1 hanging Tiffany lamp (alcove)
- 1 scissor type wall lamp (above counter)
- 1 hanging chandelier (front door)
- 1 small table lamp (piano)
- 1 wall lamp (bedroom)
- 1 wall fixture (kitchen)

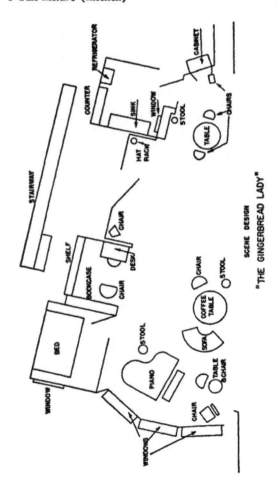

SCENE DESIGN

"THE GINGERBREAD LADY"

About the Playwright

Neil Simon began his writing career in television and established himself as our leading writer of comedy by creating a succession of Broadway hits beginning with *Come Blow Your Horn*. During the 1966-67 season, *Barefoot in the Park, The Odd Couple, Sweet Charity* and *The Star Spangled Girl* were all running simultaneously; in the 1970-71 season, Broadway theatergoers had their choice of *Plaza Suite, Last of the Red Hot Lovers* and *Promises, Promises*.

Next came *Little Me, The Gingerbread Lady, The Prisoner of Second Avenue, The Sunshine Boys, The Good Doctor, God's Favorite, They're Playing Our Song, I Ought to Be in Pictures, Fools*, a revival of *Little Me, Brighton Beach Memoirs, Biloxi Blues* (Tony Award) a new version of *The Odd Couple* starring Sally Struthers and Rita Moreno as the title duo, *Broadway Bound, Rumors, Lost in Yonkers* (Tony Award and Pulitzer Prize), *Jake's Women* and *London Suite*.

Mr. Simon has also written for the screen: the adaptations of *Barefoot in the Park, The Odd Couple, Plaza Suite, The Last of the Red Hot Lovers, The Prisoner of Second Avenue, The Sunshine Boys, California Suite, I Ought To Be In Pictures, Chapter Two, Brighton Beach Memoirs, Biloxi Blues*, the TV motion picture of *Broadway Bound* and *Lost in Yonkers*. Other screenplays he has written include *After the Fox, The Out-of-Towners, The Heartbreak Kid, Murder by Death, The Goodbye Girl, The Cheap Detective, Seems Like Old Times, Only When I Laugh, Max Dugan Returns* and *The Marrying Man*.

CPSIA information can be obtained at www.ICGtesting.com
Printed in the USA
LVOW04s1311101114

412893LV00001B/67/P